GERALD MCCRAY

Gerald McCray

WHAT IS

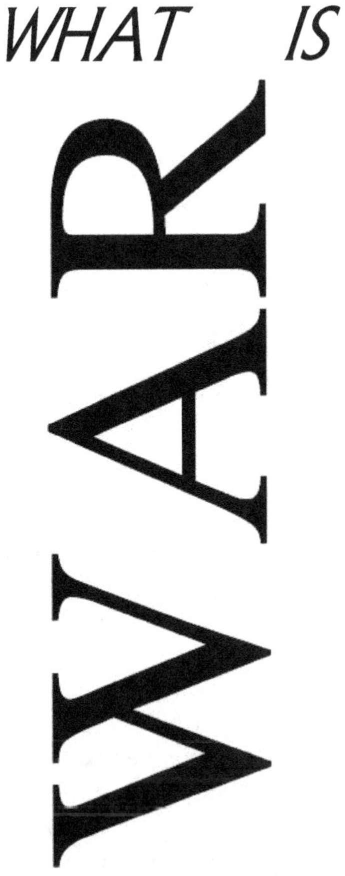

GOOD FOR?

A Sunday School Teacher Takes A Look

An Unusual Bible Study Series

What Is War Good For?

How To Heal The Warrior's Wounded Soul

A Sunday School Teacher Takes A Look

Baby Faith Publishing

ISBN-13: 978-1985070004
ISBN-10: 1985070006

DEDICATION

This book is dedicated to these heroes:

Past, present, and future soldiers who honor your uniforms and oaths by putting yourselves between the bullies which threaten freedom and the rest of us,

Soldiers who fight the "WARS" we never hear about,

Soldiers who use a single bullet to stop a WAR
before it starts,

First Responders who run to the danger so that the rest of us can run from it,

Those who struggle with TBI's, PTSD, tortured minds, and wounded souls,

The Angels we call nurses who help put the broken back together again,

And all of you unsung heroes.

WHY BIBLE STUDY?

ALL SCRIPTURE *is given by inspiration of God, and* IS PROFITABLE *for doctrine, for reproof, for correction, for instruction in righteousness,*

that the man of God may be complete, thoroughly equipped for every good work.

I charge you therefore before God and the Lord Jesus Christ, who will judge the living and the dead at His appearing and His kingdom:

Preach the word! Be ready in season and out of season. [USE THE WORD TO] *Convince, rebuke, exhort, with all longsuffering and teaching.*

For the time will come when they will not endure sound doctrine [HAVE ROOM FOR TRUTH], *but according to their own desires, because they have itching ears, they will heap up for themselves teachers;*

and they will turn their ears away from the truth, and be turned aside to fables.

2 Timothy 3:16-4:4 NKJV

CONTENTS

Dedications

A Wave Of Affection

Why Write Such A Book?

Introduction

A WAVE OF AFFECTION

This first section was the original explanation of the genesis of this book. It is maybe eleven years old.

I wrote this book for the only man [other than my son] which I've ever said, "I love you," to. The last time I talked face to face with this warrior, there was so much pain in his voice; on his face, and even the tenor of his voice. When he spoke of his tours and deployments there just seemed to be so much he wanted to say that he couldn't. He spoke in vague making sure not to violate his security clearances.

I have dealt with my own guilt and regrets enough to know what is looks like when certain cues manifest in conversations. This warrior is one of the most loving people I have ever met. We were college roommates for maybe two years if memory serves. When he fell in love, it was written all over his face. When he nailed a graphic project exactly the way he wanted to; it was written all over his face. When he came out of his devotions one day after being filled with his heavenly prayer language, it was written all over his face how excited he was about it. When he talked about his tours; deep soul pain and unquantifiable regret were written on his face.

I started writing this book within a month after we hooked up for dinner after losing touch for over seventeen years. Before we got together for dinner; we ran into each other at a movie theater. The last time I heard, he was around the world doing his duty. It was amazing and miraculous that we would run into each other while each of us were on a date with our wives. Neither of us were the touchy feely type of person when we were in college and so it was at this chance meeting. This **divine appointment**. So, we just stood there and stared at each other. Emotions were high but we were still our old selves.

I could gather from her reaction to our silence that his wife was aware of our connection so while we just stood there staring at each other without saying a word, his wife cried for us. It was a good cry.

This universal soldier [a soldier for his country as well as for his LORD] reached out to my wife about coming to the base for dinner. My wife and I were in the same campus ministry with this warrior in college so they were well acquainted. She agreed to a date and made sure I was free that day to honor the invitation. It was an amazing dinner. What an amazing cook. New foods I hadn't tried before became my new favorites.

Before departing the rendezvous, my wife and I knew we had to pray for our citizen soldier. The pain, angst, and regret of military duty were weighing heavy on my friend. My brother. I deliberately held conversations with former combat marines specifically looking for reasons why the burden is so heavy on combat soldiers and "secret conflict" veterans. They all agree that the pain, regret, angst, and depression arise from survivors' remorse as well as the harm they have inflicted on others rather than the trauma and injury they have personally sustained.

I met a marine who suffered a traumatic brain injury and was in dire straits for years. His brain was wounded by someone else but that wounding didn't touch his soul. What he did to harm others did touch his soul...deeply. When affable people with a decent conscience hurt others, they also wound their own souls. What was written on my roommate's face was obvious. What he had to do to cope in foreign lands as well as carry out his duty wounded his soul. Once I noticed the cues, I knew what I had to do. He refused the encouragement and "absolution" which my wife and I offered him during our after dinner conversation.

I knew there was some encouragement in the Word of Almighty Most High God which could heal this warrior's wounded soul, mind, and heart. So, I started writing the best I could. A head injury which I sustained on the job put this book and several other manuscripts on hold for nearly twelve years. One day, the switch flipped and I came crawling back a paragraph at a time. I don't have the words to convey my personal regret and sorrow for not being able to finish this work sooner.

Sticks and stones can break my bones but....blah...blah...blah. Words can and will hurt. Words can also heal. The Word of the Living God is especially designed to heal according to Psalm 107:20, Luke 7:7, and Revelation 12:11. According to Hebrews 4:12, the Word of the Living God is the only scalpel that exists which can cut along the dividing line of soul and spirit. It can differentiate between the two parts of the human construct which we think are one and the same. If Almighty Most High God's Word is that exacting; then it can also excise the soul wounds which nothing else can help.

Why did I write this book?

In hopes of healing my friend's wounded soul and hopefully those of other warriors..

Why Write Such A Book?

Over twelve years ago I sustained a head injury while working in a warehouse. Before the incident, I had several manuscripts I was working on. One was entitled *Healing The Soldier's Wounded Heart.* That is why I am writing this book. When the necessity to push back against the global bullies is taught in it's proper Biblical perspective, our wounded warriors can find peace and healing even in light of atrocious images which haunt them constantly.

You should defend those who cannot help themselves.   Proverbs 31:8 TLB

I saw what I surmised as unfathomable pain, regret, and condemnation in the eyes of former combat soldiers for years. It reminded me of what I saw in my Dad's eyes as I was growing up. At the time it was indescribable. After communicating with former combat soldiers, I finally understood what it was − pain on multiple levels. Pain which tainted his voice. Maybe even a tortured soul. I couldn't write even one chapter following the head injury until about late 2016 - early 2017. Now, it is time to finish what I started. Because the church hasn't handled the subject of war properly [from a Biblical Truth perspective], soldiers are burdened with regret and their souls are wounded by the aftermath of what they did while following orders. The TRUTH truly will make them free as Jesus said in John 8:32. "Made free" sounds so much better than set free. A state of freedom comes from the inside out. Regardless of the external conditions, once Jesus MAKES YOU FREE you are truly free indeed!

One former combat Marine shared a very intriguing thought with me many years ago. He said that physically wounded soldiers dealing with PSTD are usually impacted more by what they did to others rather than what damage has been done to them and their bodies. A tortured soul cannot be remedied by modern medicine. No amount of medical care can touch the soul. No regimen of physical therapy and neuroleptics can ever be aggressive enough to sooth a tortured soul. The Word of Almighty Most High God CAN PERFORM SURGERY ON THE SOUL. It can soothe what ails the soul. No one else and nothing else can.

Hebrews 4:12 says that God's Word can cut along the dividing line between soul and spirit. We hear the terms "soul" and "spirit" used so interchangeably that we think that soul and spirit are one and the same but the Word of God knows the difference and it can excise the wounds of the soul. It can excise the wounds of the mind. It can put you at peace as though it never happened at all. If you study the New Testament regarding the subjects of grace, justification, sanctification, and righteousness; you will come to the conclusion that Our Heavenly Father wants to treat us as if sin never happened. Like we never did anything wrong. WOW!

If the church had been teaching about WAR accurately, then soldiers could have been better equipped to deal with the wounds of their minds and souls long before they were inflicted. The blood of Jesus' cross can heal any wound of the spirit, soul, mind, emotions or body. He wants to heal you. According to 1st Peter 2:24, He already has healed you. Healed all of us on *The* Cross. The promises of Almighty Most High God are like a contract [or covenant even] which we need to familiarize ourselves with. We will find that we are leaving many benefits on the table.(Psalm 23:5) Let's find out what His Word says about us. When we do, we only need to accept it, believe it, and receive it with our mouths. Simply by saying, "Yes Jesus, yes!" Just talk to Him. You will find the right words. Thank God for His Son Jesus, thank Jesus for His cross, blood, and name. Ask Father God to make you His child, and thank Him for healing you, "JUST AS YOU SAID IN YOUR

WORD," and keep thanking Him for the rest of your life.

To be clear, I am not pro war. I am pro truth. Truth, according to Jesus, makes us free. The truth about God makes us free. The truth about faith and grace makes us free. According to Jesus Himself, the Word of God is the spiritually cleansing truth. (John 17:17) If church people ignore the truth then they forfeit the spiritual cleansing which God's Word offers. The Word of God is spiritually cleansing water according to Ephesians 5:26. If we misuse and mishandle the Word we can muddy the waters and put ourselves in jeopardy of not being free indeed.

GOOD

minus GO D

equals   O

Your unbiblical opinion can be deadly. For example, "All roads lead to God," is a supposition some erroneously take hold of and they do so to their detriment. Final judgment is the only destination where all roads converge. If all roads lead to God then I really don't need God. I simply must try my best to be good. Or at least better than the next guy. The spiritual danger of attempting to be good without God is we are left with an absolute zero.

One critical understanding the church misses is that faith (or lack thereof) is a matter of life and death to anyone. Spiritual life to the believer or spiritual death to the wicked. *"God said it, I believe it, and that settles,"* it is a common adage in certain ecumenical circles. It is an amazing affirmation of the truth of God's Word. All of God's Word! Still, when we preach, teach or talk about particular social and geopolitical issues in these ecumenical arenas, we more often than not spout generally accepted social sentiment rather than what *The* Truth - the Word of Almighty Most High God - actually says.

Disagreeing with the Word of Truth (John 1:14, John 17:17, 2nd Cor. 6:7, Eph. 1:13, Col. 1:15, 2nd Tim. 2:15, James 1:18) has a consequential impact on our faith. Believing something opposite of what the Word says is believing wrong or scripturally called *"unbelief."* I mean, who would argue that WAR is a bad thing? But the detriment to faith is teaching that is contrary to what the Word of Almighty Most High God actually says. *What Is War Good For?* may come across as pro war but keep in mind that truth is truth even if you disagree with it. Even if you want the opposite to be true. Such as where all roads end up.

Still, the question, "what is war good for?" intrigued me enough to answer the question. One pastor recruited me as a Sunday School superintendent when I was about seventeen years old. Another pastor tricked me into writing my first book after asking me to develop a Bible Study regarding women in ministry. I have been putting my Bible Studies in book form ever since. Maybe it was a God trick. Hmmm. This is an interesting Bible Study. War of all things? Who would have thought?

Charles Edwin Hatcher asked a rhetorical question with his poplar Vietnam War protest song entitled WAR. The question was and is, "what is war good for?" Hatcher went on to answer the question with, "*Absolutely nothing!*" The problem is Hatcher got it wrong. Barrett Strong and Norman Whitfield who wrote for the Motown record label are credited with writing this song. The lyrics reflected the sentiment of the public at large. Most civilized people felt exactly the same way Hatcher did.

Even the church echoed Hatcher's sentiments and to this day still does. The fact of the matter is that most of the church got it wrong as well. The post modern church, as usual, got its position from the world system rather than from the Word of Truth. That is the usual genesis of apostasy. Those who identify themselves as God's people fail to get their world view from God's Word. As ambassadors of The

Anointed One (2nd Corinthians 5:20), we are not to speak our own opinions but only the words of our King, Potentate or government. We church people and Christians too often break with diplomatic protocol and speak our own minds rather than what our King has instructed in His Word – His articles of engagement.

Our ignorance of the Word makes us perfect fodder for the secular, humanistic, and antithetical propaganda which is being spued out of hostile media outlets. The anti-Jehovah, anti-Jesus, anti-Christian, and anti-Bible platitudes and veiled insults constantly and aggressively flow from the mouths of entertainment news personalities. If they interject themselves into the news cycle long enough, they just may become entertainment news celebrities (E NC). The old fashioned investigative reporter has disappeared from the marketplace or been given a propaganda make over. **Truth has no place** in news coverage anymore. Innuendo, deceptive allegations, and pungent pundit opinions are now the order of the day. The saddest part of all of this is that the church world drinks in this sludge like eager hatchlings waiting for momma bird to regurgitate into their mouths. The new format for broadcast news is diametrically opposed to that which made anchor men and women trusted household names for decades. Now, we get media outlets colluding with anti-Christian entities to lynch pin the outcome of elections in favor of anti-Christian social agendas. AND the church people of America are in lock step formation. God have mercy!

Anyway, as a Bible Study and Sunday School Teacher for several years; I have gone through the Holy Scriptures many times and have developed a perspective of the subject of war which is completely opposite of the way the subject has been taught in some church arenas. Too many teachers of the Word fail to ask the right questions regarding their personal views of Bible subjects. Yes, Bible subjects. Church people have views on issues such as WAR and capital punishment based on how they "feel" about the issues as well as how the anti-God, anti-Jesus, and anti-Bible media outlets frame the issues with their deceptive secularly apologetics.

In the world of diplomacy, the diplomat's or ambassador's "feelings" on a particular issue are completely irrelevant. To do their job the way they are supposed to, they leave their feelings and opinions out of the conversation while interacting with leaders of other nations and simply use the words which their king, prime minister or president give them to use.

This Bible Study is not for everyone. Proceed with caution if you are not a fan of the whole truth.

It will be brief though. No need to spend much time on this subject. I simply want to make the clarion point that the Word says something completely different from what the serpent's people say. Listening to the lie could make you vulnerable. Maybe even a victim. WAR is not something anyone wishes for but it is a necessity. Now, if you were being crushed under the weight of the totalitarian rule of some evil despot, you might long for or even pray for a stronger yet benevolent ruler to liberate you. It just may take WAR to make that happen. Would you still want to be free?

Would still want to be rescued from your monsters? Or continue to agree with Hatcher that WAR is good for absolutely nothing?

IN THE MOVIES there are multiple renditions of monsters but in nature there is only one monster – humans. Genetically re-engineered dinosaurs go on a wildlife killing rampage and are said to be, "killing for sport." Animals kill to eat or to defend. There are no monsters in the animal kingdom past or present which kill for sport. The only monster in nature is mankind itself. The sin nature (Romans chapter 6) has made monsters of us all to some degree but make no mistake. Because of the sin nature, we all have the same seeds which Hitler, Stalin, Idi Amin, Slobodan Milosevic, and the Butcher of Bakersfield have or had in them. The Word of Most High God warns of the monsters who wish to ruler over others. It tells us of the aggressive violent nature of those categorized in the scriptures as wicked [twisted] thinkers.

One reason Noah's flood judgment came on the world was to abate the exponential increase of violence and WAR according to the sixth chapter of Genesis.   A well known quote from 18th century British parliament member Edmund Burke is a perfect example of the conflict which Jesus' Cross, blood, and name put an end to – the hostility between the Most High God and humanity's sin nature. The nature of the monster.

"The only thing necessary for the triumph of evil is for good men to do nothing."   Edmund Burke

The ultimate good man – GodMan – Jesus – waged WAR on the kingdom of darkness to retrieve what that monster force stole – the souls of humanity. Jesus began His ministry in the fourth chapter of Luke with a declaration of WAR of sorts with:

The Spirit of the Most High is upon Me because He has empowered me TO SET *the spiritual* CAPTIVES, *economic captives, social captives, health captives, genetic captives, brokenhearted captives, and [tortured souls]* FREE.   Luke 4:18

Jesus was not like some flower child whispering at the airport. He made the declaration of WAR loud and clear. The fact that the Master Wordsmith uses the term "captives" means that someone was being held in a situation or condition AGAINST THEIR WILL. The problem with the captivity in which every person in history except for Jesus finds themselves in is so stealthy that we erroneously consider ourselves free.

I mean, why wouldn't we? We come and go as we please. We enter our closet at will and decide what to wear. We decide to marry or not to. Why would we agree that we are captives.   THIS SPIRITUAL CAPTIVITY is a bondage we were all born into as a result of the first family's fall from grace in Eden's garden. It is a captivity and bondage of the spirit, soul, mind, and emotions.

31 To the Jews who had believed him, Jesus said, "If you hold to my teaching, you are really my disciples. 32 Then you will know the truth, and the truth will set you free."

33 They answered him, "We are Abraham's descendants and have never been slaves of anyone. How can you say that we shall be set free?"

John 8:31-33 NIV

Still don't think that you are in bondage? This kind of captivity convinces you that you are free. Even that you have never been in bondage of any kind. The religious leadership of Jesus ' day were adamant about never having been in bondage ever. I guess no one told them about and Assyrian (722 B.C.) and Babylonian (586 B.C.) captivities not to mention that they went into Egypt with less than a hundred people and came out of that slavery four hundred years later with three to nearly six million souls. Regardless of the history, they denied ever being in bondage.

We are the same way today. We are in denial of the captivity we find ourselves in. We call the derivatives of our captivity "lifestyle choices." The killing of over 75 million unborn children in what should be the safest place in the world as a form of contraception isn't seen as captivity but a lifestyle choice. Every choice is a seed and this one has resulted in several bitter harvests. Let's name a few. The continual increases in the costs of higher education is one. The incessant search by progressives to find for more ways to tax the American people into abject oppression.

Ever increasing taxes on gasoline, online shopping, and communications cartels (paid television) are all linked together. Hitler's holocaust of six million Jewish people destroyed a couple to a few generations of Almighty Most High God's chosen people. The American Utero Holocaust, on the other hand, has annihilated generations upon generations of college students. More college students could result in lower educational costs and financial aid for those who otherwise couldn't attend.

The WAR on the womb has destroyed future great great grandmothers. Maybe that is why modesty is one of many lost virtues. Fewer and fewer grandmothers mentoring future generations of mentors. The sin nature deceives us into thinking that these horrors are our choice when the Word of Almighty Most High God makes it crystal clear that without Christ Jesus transforming our dead human spirits by the power of HIS cross; we are slaves to that altogether deceptive sin nature.

The sin nature - the nature of the serpent - is so deeply embedded within us (Romans 6), that we think the "rationally" devised solutions we come up with are civilized. I guess the ancient Egyptian worshippers of the falcon head god Horus thought it was civilized to lay their infants onto the burning arms of Horus' statue. **On the contrary,** we are as evil as the suicide radicals or the ethnic cleansing despots because the sin nature is the nature of our devilish and hellish captor. Romans 5:12 tells us that we inherited the sin nature from the first parents just as we did the genetic material from our immediate parents. That is a tough bondage and slavery which is impossible to escape. ON OUR OWN. We needed a much stronger ruler (Matt. 12:29 Mark 3:27 Luke 11:21) to come and rescue us.

Jesus threw down the gauntlet with His first public sermon (Luke 4) putting the kingdom of darkness (Luke 22:53/Colossians 1:13) on notice that He was coming and bringing -Heaven's power with Him to set the captives free. He let the monster kingdom of darkness know that He was coming to defeat them and to rescue the oppressed, vulnerable, and defenseless. Because Almighty Most High God responded in kind to the Snake of Eden and won the WAR for humanity's souls, we CAN BE redeemed! This choice is an easy one.

Look at more of Jesus' discourse with the religious leaders who were convinced that their people had never been slaves to anyone:

34 Jesus replied, "I tell you the truth, everyone who

sins is a slave to sin.
35 Now a slave has no permanent place in the family, but a son belongs to it forever.
36 So if the Son sets you free, you will be free indeed.
37 I know you are Abraham's descendants. Yet you are ready to kill me, because you have no room for my word.   John 8:34-37 NIV

The captivity and bondage from which Jesus came to set us free is not obvious. It is in the unseen realm. Sin is invisible. We can't see sin. We can see the physical exhibitions of sinful deeds and motivations. The acts of sin themselves are closely related to sin but the evil rationale which comes out of us is coming from what a summary view of Romans 6 could term *The Sin Nature*.

The sin nature or nature of the serpent (Revelation 20:2) IS THE CAPTIVITY we are born into. Jesus will free us if we accept His rescue and trade the nature of the serpent for the divine nature of the Lamb of God. (John 6:53-58/2nd Peter 1:3-4/Revelation 1:5-6) As a slave to the serpent, you have no hope. But if you accept Jesus' free grace offer of rescue from your spiritual captivity, you will finally be made free indeed and placed into the family of the Almighty Most High God the Creator and Father of The Lord Yeshua Jesus.

That's right!

We Are Redeemed by Jesus winning the WAR, binding and stripping our monster captive of his power, and opening our prison doors. Just as WAR against Nazi Germany freed those who were oppressed and prevented others from being oppressed by those monsters, Jesus' cross, blood, and name free whoever will accept His rescue and walk out of the cells and from under the oppression.

See?

I told you this would be a brief Bible Study. For those who are convinced that *wrongly believing* what the Word of Almighty God says can be dangerous to our spiritual wellbeing, then this Bible Study is over for you. For those of you who need a bit more informative and transforming truth to make the point as well as some soul healing, feel free to turn the page.

Introduction

Whenever I have heard a discussion on WAR by church folk and non-church folk alike, I have nearly always heard, "Jesus did say to love one another didn't He?" A statement to that effect is thrown out to settle an argument between those with the dove mentalities and those with the hawk mentalities. The problem with this stance is it attempts to apply what Jesus was speaking of in one arena to a completely different one.

Yes, Jesus did say to love one another but for nearly 30 years He also instructed Joshua and the Israelites in WAR. Joshua's name was changed from Oshea which means "help" to Yehoshua which means "Jehovah's help" or Jehovah's salvation. **God helped Joshua to war?** In this politically correct sensitivity training era I know that such a statement that can be considered divisive. The fact remains that during Joshua's leadership, thirty one kings and six nations were defeated. Joshua defeated every army he fought.

So, if Almighty Most High God helped in WAR and WAR should be condemned according to some people who simply repeat common media and social sentiments; should the Most High be condemned? Put on trial for war crimes even? After all, Jesus did say to love everyone...didn't He?   I remember a bit of the Old Testament war stories my pastors have told over the years of how God instructed certain people like Joshua, Gideon, and David in battle. Would these same preachers also condemn war as well? Some do never really putting war in the proper biblical perspective.   Maybe we can better understand war from its accurate Biblical perspective.

Just reading the title of this book quickly brings to mind the most memorable lyrics of a popular song from the late sixties protesting the Vietnam War. War sentiment was extremely high and though this song didn't start Charles Edwin Hatcher's career it is credited with cementing it in making him a "Motown legend." In fact, the song was so popular that Hatcher included it on two of his albums.   For younger readers trying to understand the term *"albums,"* imagine gigantic black plastic compact discs. They were too big to play on a computer.

Many Americans were against the WAR and for good reason. The images of WAR which came back to the states via television and photos put the stark reality and harshness of WAR right in our faces. We saw what carnage and devastation was left behind in war's wake and wanted to do whatever we could to stop it. We wanted this *"senseless killing"* to stop and we wanted it to stop right now. Many political operatives, social power brokers, Hollywood celebrities, and musicians threw their hats in the ring and made their opinions known. Some did so to the detriment of their careers and relationships. Remember what's-her-name?

Anti-war sentiment was so prevalent and impassioned that some opponents of the war lambasted the soldiers and mistreated them when they returned home. Spitting on soldiers and labeling them as "baby killers" was the reception many soldiers received. Anti-war sentiment gave birth to so much hatred that decades had to pass before our Vietnam veterans were finally welcomed home. Even then, individual states rather than the federal government took the lead in organizing the welcome home parades. One of the most popular and enduring ways of protesting the war was through music and Charles Edwin Hatcher [aka Edwin Starr] offered the anti war crowd an anthem that is still popular today. Hatcher posed some very poignant questions and made some undeniable observations with his lyrics.

WAR! - It ain't nothing but a heartbreaker,
WAR! - Friend only to the undertaker.

WAR is an enemy to all mankind,
The thought of war blows my mind.
WAR has caused unrest within the younger generation
Induction then destruction...who wants to die?

Hatcher's song was so popular because it made so much sense. Who would disagree that WAR is bad? His lyrics resounded in the minds of everyone. I was only ten years old when the U.S. embassy in Saigon fell but I understood the concept of bullies as well as the consequences of ignoring them. These lessons were learned from the bullies at school, in the neighborhood, and at home. We know that if the path to war is traveled too long that eventually we will destroy one another. It does blow the mind that violence of any kind including domestic violence, bullying of any kind, and war even exist. I mean why is war a reality of life? Can we just do away with it all together? Is it possible for us to all get along and love one another like Jesus said? Good questions.

Hatcher's song answered the rhetorical question of war's necessity with, "absolutely nothing!" The problem with that answer is Hatcher got it completely wrong. Again, I am not pro-war; only pro truth. The truth of Almighty Most High God's Word teaches that the salvation of souls was accomplished by WAR. The tenth chapter of Daniel is one of the scriptures which give us a glimpse into the fact that WAR began and continues in the unseen realm. A WAR raging nearly since the beginning of time for the gain or loss of the souls of humanity.

One of the things I have learned from surveying the Bible is that violence and war did not begin in this realm. I have been a Sunday School teacher for some time now and just happened to have come across the issue of war from a Biblical perspective in my studies and find it quite difficult to reconcile the war sentiment we hear in the media and churches with how the Bible handles war.

Yes, I said the Bible. It is the Owner's manual for life and living and applies to every realm of man's existence. To be clear and politically incorrect, the Owner I refer to is God - the Creator God - whom the Bible says is the Father of the Lord Jesus Christ. In my study of the scriptures I just didn't recall reading where Jesus condemned war. Even the iconic King David fell into adulterous and murderous behavior because he wasn't at WAR as he was scheduled to be. To be honest, I have never looked at the scriptures for the specific subject of war but in my few years of reading and studying the Bible I just couldn't recall reading a blatant condemnation of war. To be clear, the Owner is God the Creator and the

Bible is His manual given to us. He gave us His Word in print so that we would know how He thinks and to know the way we should think.

THAT GOT ME THINKING. Now if Jesus didn't condemn war [if I am correct] then why do His people? He said that His people hear His voice and will not respond to the voice of another shepherd. Another spirit. So, why do so many "Jesus people" condemn war when He didn't? I think the obvious answer to that question is that Jesus' people don't understand WAR the way Jesus does.

Do we understand that getting God into a human body for the purpose of redeeming mankind was WAR?

Do we understand that keeping His silence during the mock trials leading up to the crucifixion was WAR?

Do we understand that praying in Gethsemane to the point of sweating drops of blood was WAR?

Far too many "Jesus people" don't have an accurate Biblical perspective of war. And far too many "Jesus people" misunderstand what *the real Jesus* meant when He talked about loving one another.

Far too many church people condemn war on the basis of Jesus' sermon on the mountainside recorded in Matthew chapters 5,6, and 7 as well as Luke chapter 6 in which He instructed His listeners to, "...love your enemies..." Applying this instruction to the horrible reality of and potential for war is dangerous and uniformed. If this instruction applies to war then God's Word in Romans 13:3-4 completely contradicts it when it tells us that evildoers have to be punished by others whose callings involve dealing with those who would hurt others.

According to Romans 13:3-4, those whose duty it is to protect the common welfare are authorized by the Supreme Authority of Creation to do the punishing. Capital punishment was not introduced to humanity by men but by God in His warnings in 14 of the first 15 books of the Bible. Still, church people agree with humanistic sentiment to abolish capital punishment because we should love everyone. Because it is not fair. Many say that it should be abolished because, "it is not a deterrent." Almighty Most High God didn't implement punishment as a deterrent but as a punishment.

Far too many Christians misunderstand and thus erroneously apply Jesus' instructions to love and forgive. Relationships throughout humanity have many levels such as interpersonal, social, civil, political, economic, occupational, legal, national, international, and global.   I have talked with too many church people who attempt to apply Jesus' *"love-and-forgive"* instructions to issues such as war and capital punishment. They don't realize that they are applying Jesus' interpersonal standards of conduct, love, and forgiveness to levels of human relationship to which they were not intended. Still, these church people insist that their unbiblical worldview is correct.

So, when 15 Saudis, 1 Lebanese, 1 Egyptian, and 2 citizens from the United Arab Emirates together killed over 2,800 people on September 11, 2001 should we just have "loved our enemies" and just let it go? If we had then we would have violated the generally accepted principles ensuring the common welfare and justice as well as scriptural imperatives such as Romans 13:4.

For good reason Jesus said in Luke 16:8 that the children of darkness are smarter than the Children of Light. There must be a clearer understanding that reconciles Jesus' instructions on love in the New Testament with His instructions to war in the Old Testament as Pastors have been teaching their churches for centuries. Children in ankle biter church choirs singing, "Joshua fought the battle of Jericho," with jovial inflections and joyous smiles come to mind. The church seemed to have had a much better understanding of WAR forty years ago than it does now. What about our understanding has changed?

So, I decided to take a journey through the scriptures surveying the Word on the subject of WAR. Now, I invite you to take this journey as well and see what we find. The closer we get to the next election the more it concerns me that Christians will hand over the reins of power to those who will mishandle the terror threat because they believe that a diplomatic solution is feasible although the Word says there is none. "Let's just talk," is what I hear from too many candidates who simply reflect certain social segments. Is there a diplomatic solution to a religious belief? "Wiping Israel off the face of the earth" and "death to America" are not statements born out of ideological disputes or political differences but a deep seeded religious belief. A belief of hatred.

Hatred for America and the hell bent to annihilate the Jewish people is not an ideology but is deep in the blood. Hatred first and foremost for Almighty Most High God -the Creator- is focused on anything and anyone who represents HIM. Israel's robust existence following eons of WAR, captivity, slavery, constant threats by hostile nations which outnumber Jews 70:1

is an undeniable miracle.   Destroying Israel would disprove ALL the Bible verses where the Most High God promises everlasting existence to Israel.   The hatred against Israel is hatred against *The* Creator, *The* Christ, and *The* Cross.   This hatred runs deep.   Deep in the unexplored fathoms of the soul. There is no magnitude of threat, show of force, or diplomatic nonsense that can deal with this ail. The hatred and vitriol aimed at the followers of the *True and Living God* have brewed since about 2079 B.C. (Hagar/Ismail) and its simmering boil is nearing the tipping point.   Or detonation.

You ready for this journey?   Let's go.

Chapter One

Thank You Soldiers!

And here is how to measure it-the greatest love is shown when a person lays down his life for his friends

John 15:13 TLB

Many years ago, I participated in an email circle in which we encouraged spiritual, economic, and social growth. My former college roommate was also in that email circle. One day I noticed that most of the recipients of his messages were military personnel. When I noticed all of the military email addresses, I just had to honor our soldiers by sending them a letter of gratitude for their service and sacrifice to our nation and the world. My Dad was a Korean War veteran whose forearm was so damaged that pins, rods, and screws were used to put that forearm back together. My Dad died during my freshman year in college. I didn't know him that well. He was cold and distant. Maybe that is why I am cold and distant. Talking to combat veterans about their experiences helped me better understand my Dad. On his death bed, I was instructed to say, "I love you," to him but I failed that test and didn't heed those instructions. Sending a message to these military email recipients was me also sending a message to my Dad. I could finally say through this email message, "I love you Daddy."

It went something like this:

I am not military but when I noticed the "mil" extensions on so many of these email addresses, I had to send all of you a message of thanks. During

Operation Desert Storm, I saw a uniformed soldier in the supermarket once and asked to shake his hand because he represented all of you brave men and women [and my Dad] to me. In that moment, I felt like I was shaking the hands of thousands of soldiers. I finally shook my Dad's hand for the first time in my life.

Some Capitol Hill embeds try to politicize you soldiers but rest assured that you are so much more to God. So much more. Psalm 15:4 and Romans 13:4 come to mind when I consider the type of person who puts himself or herself in harm's way to ensure the domestic tranquility of those who don't or can't. The person who keeps their oath of duty even in the face of personal harm and even death has a special place in the presence of Almighty God according to Psalm 15:4. Now, reading the entire fifteenth Psalm gives the ideal picture of what a *Soldier of The Cross* should be. Romans 13:4 tells us that every agent of a legitimate policing force (whether domestic or global) is a servant of Almighty God enforcing standards of righteousness punishing those who violate HIS laws of conduct. WOW!

When I shook the soldier's hand in the supermarket, I thought about my college roommate as well. We joked a couple of times about him being America's last hope as a continuing democracy. I knew from the pain my father, a Korean WAR veteran, carried with him to his death bed that it is no joke. You guys have volunteered and vowed to lay down your lives so that freedom can continue to ring loud and clear. What if America had ignored the reports of German aggression in Europe and never strategized and implemented Operation Overlord (Normandy, France) which resulted in a victory we civilians call "D-day?" Would the schools in France be teaching mandatory German? Would Britain's Union Jack have been replace by a modified swastika? Would America's national anthem have been changed by Austrian-Jew Adolf Hitler? Yes, we lost over thirty four thousand American soldiers in Normandy but those soldier's sacrifices liberated France from the monster invaders.

Ladies, I mean no disrespect when I say "guys" because you are also the guys protecting freedom around the world. Galatians chapter 3 tells us that freedom is a gift which God gave to all people. When you guys defend freedom or liberate oppressed peoples, you are in eternally good company if you choose. Jesus' first sermon was a proclamation of spiritual, social, mental, and class emancipation. Slavery, oppression, and murder are the blight which Satan put on mankind when he tricked Adam and Eve into surrendering their authority and power over the earth. (Genesis calls it dominion) The blessing which our Creator spoke over the human race was now under the control of the adversary and twisted to work against us. Adam surrendered his authority and power into the hands of a malevolent being who is hell bent on destroying humanity just to get back at Creator God. For being better than he.

As soldiers, you all know firsthand what chaos would result if your superiors surrendered their authority and power into the hands and control of some despotic nation which wants nothing more than the destruction of America. Some erroneously think that destroying America would make Israel a sitting duck. Almighty Most High God has been protecting Israel long before Abraham Lincoln invited Jews to come in droves to America. The 1951 Mutual Friendship Agreement between America and Israel benefits America more than it does Israel. Most High God protected Israel long before America existed and would do the same if this superpower was not a friend of Israel. Even if America was in league with Israel's most hostile enemies laying siege to the City of Peace; Israel would still have the advantage. God's promises.

Imagine   an   anti-American   political   operative somehow weaseling into the oval office [with the ballot box assistance of wayward Catholics and sideline Evangelicals] and dismantling the republic from the inside out? What would that look like? Attacking our religious foundations? Mandating anti-conscience clauses forcing those in the medical field to do unrighteous deeds which violate their moral, religious, Biblical, and spiritual beliefs? Would he/she secretly fund blatant terrorist nations which have vowed to destroy America and wipe Israel off the face of the earth?

What would the legacy of such a president be who would fund the destruction of God's Prince - Israel? The fifteenth verse of Obadiah's prophecy says that what it done to Israel shall be repaid on the perpetrators. Maybe a non political operative is what we need. The career politicians have nearly destroyed this nation. They politicize soldiers rather than honor and care for them as we should for protecting freedom around the world. Protecting freedom around the world is helping the Disciples' prayer request, "Thy kingdom come," come to pass. The Word of God speaks of special grace given to police forces to accomplish their objectives. I am convinced that special protection is given to those who remain under authority as well.

Psalm 15 calls what you guys do, *swearing to your*

own hurt and not changing your actions even if you change your mind. Because God is a "Man" of His Word, He rushes to watch over His Word to perform it according to Jeremiah 1:12. I am convinced that He also is anxious to protect those who keep their word even in the face of death.

My Dad lived for years in so much pain. Yes, he was wounded and had many surgeries on his arm which pained him frequently but his greatest pain was in his soul. He tried to soothe that pain in sordid ways and with sordid people over the years. He fought at the behest of his country long before the Civil Rights laws and acts were realized. Black soldiers were shot in the back by white Americans who were supposed to watch their backs. America has so much to atone for where the Black warrior is concerned. I did not come close to understanding my Dad's pain until recent years after having talks with former combat Marines. My Dad had to live with the images, memories, pain, and guilt of Korea. I don't want any of you to have to live like that. You can get rid of it the same way he did. Accepting Jesus' plan, purpose, and position for his life. He found that accepting the grace of Jesus' cross was the only salve that could soothe his soul.

There are two ruling spirits in the world-God and Satan. Everyone works for one or the other. Those protecting freedom have to use the same techniques as those threatening freedom. My father was under authority and in Korea to help. Still, he was damaged to his soul at the techniques which he had to use to help others.

5 So I said: "Woe is me, for I am undone! Because I am a man of unclean lips, And I dwell in the midst of a people of unclean lips; For my eyes have seen the King, The Lord of hosts."
6 Then one of the seraphim flew to me, having in his hand a live coal which he had taken with the tongs from the altar.
7 And he touched my mouth with it, and said: "Behold, this has touched your lips; Your iniquity is taken away, And your sin purged."   Isaiah 6:5-7

I am pleased to say that my Dad received God's remedy for his pain. The fire of Almighty Most High God's holy altar can cleanse the heart and mind of any stain and heal any wounded soul.   The blood of Jesus washed him clean of his sin nature and gave peace to the memories. He still looked so strong the last time I saw him leading him to the Lord. Two weeks later, he passed into eternity...in peace. All of those years of pain didn't end until he invited God into his pain.

He will wipe away all tears from their eyes, and there shall be no more death, nor sorrow, nor crying, nor pain. All of that has gone forever."

Revelation 21:4 TLB

You don't have to wait that long for peace. Jesus is waiting for your call. He said in Psalm 91 that He would be with us in our pain and trouble and deliver us. Receive God's peace, let it go, and move on with God. Some of you may never have to deal with this issue. The same grace that delivers those who do keeps others from having to experience it. Either way, know that God is with you everywhere you go. He already knows what you have done. He knows what you are going to do. Because Jesus lived in the flesh, He knows how you are feeling. Hebrews 4:15-16 tells us that Jesus knows what it is like to be us.

15 Our High Priest is not one who cannot feel sympathy for our weaknesses. On the contrary, we have a High Priest who was tempted in every way that we are, but did not sin.
16 Let us have confidence, then, and approach God's throne, where there is grace. There we will receive mercy and find grace to help us just when we need it.

Hebrews 4:15-16 TEV

He understands the hurt, pain, and even fear. Yes,

Jesus understands fear. He knows what it is like to be us. Even to be you. He was abandoned on *The Cross* and the only right One in worst part of Hell while the Old Testament saints watched from the safety of Paradise (also called Abraham's Bosom). He endured combat for the souls of humanity and He even conducted a Trump Processional in which He stripped the principalities, rulers of darkness, spiritual wickedness in high places, and the serpent of all their stripes, power, and authority according to Colossians 2:12-15.

12 buried with Him in baptism, in which you also were raised with Him through faith in the working of God, who raised Him from the dead.
13 And you, being dead in your trespasses and the uncircumcision of your flesh, He has made alive together with Him, having forgiven you all trespasses,
14 having wiped out the handwriting of requirements that was against us, which was contrary to us. And He has taken it out of the way, having nailed it to the cross.
15 Having disarmed principalities and powers, He made a public spectacle of them, triumphing over them in it.   Colossians 2:12-15

Jesus' beatings, death, burial, and resurrection was absolute WAR. Absolute hell. And because He trumped the kingdom of darkness, we are redeemed. Yes, redeemed by WAR. In the same way our soldiers have helped liberate oppressed nations and ethnic groups the world over; Jesus' combat has resulted in the liberation of our oppressed and imprisoned dead human spirit cores. That information does us no good unless we reach out with our hearts, minds, and mouths and simply accept what Jesus has done for us.

Call Him and give it to Him. You don't have to carry it one more minute. I have a tendency to ramble so I will stop here. Know this: You are not alone.

ONE SOLDIER'S RESPONSE:

I don't know why I'm just now reading this today. WOW.

A SUPER SOLDIER'S RESPONSE:

Hi Josie,

Yes, "WOW" is a little word, but my good friend, Gerald McCray, is a man full of God's spirit and power, a dynamite speaker, and an author. He has just rewritten his first book, "*God's Gals*." Yes, we were roommates at Virginia Tech and members of a number of God-centered organizations. He currently has two other books in the works. He is currently a member of First Agape Baptist Community of Faith in Alexandria, Virginia. A Bible believing, Bible teaching, Jesus loving church"

My former roommate was being much too kind in his assessment of me but he is the main reason I wrote this book. Because I eventually understood the pain of my father's soul many years after he passed away, I quickly noticed it in the eyes of my former roommate when we ran into each other at a movie theater maybe some 22 years after college. No matter what scriptures I could have recited, it is alone time with the Word itself that can help heal a wounded "tortured" soul. Wounded souls need to meditate on the specific scriptures which will change their mindset about whatever they are dealing with. Deep wounds which can only be reached by the Word of the Living God. His Word knows the dividing line between spirit and soul. That means it can cut out those things which wound, scar, and attach themselves to our souls. Only God can reach in and heal that soul hurt. Invite Him to do just that.

The Lord is close to the brokenhearted; he rescues those whose spirits are crushed. Psalms 34:18 NLT

The sacrifice you desire is a broken spirit. You will not

reject a broken and repentant heart, O God.
Psalms 51:17 NLT

3 To everything there is a season, and a time to every purpose under the heaven:
8 A time to love, and a time to hate; a time of war, and a time of peace.   Ecclesiastes 3:1,8

War has a time and place. Soldiering has a time and place.   The need for warriors cannot be denied. Bullies must be met with overwhelming force to abate the aggression. Yeshua Jesus took on the kingdom of darkness which had the souls of humanity enslaved in death, trespasses, and sins (Ephesians 2:1) and has opened the cells of the imprisoned and obliterated the walls.   When He preached His first sermon following the wilderness temptation, He announced that He was anointed by the Holy Spirit to make people whole on multiple dimensions. Spirit, soul, , mind, emotions, and body.

51

Chapter Two

WAR?

In Heaven?

Then there was WAR in heaven. Michael and the angels under his command fought the dragon and his angels. And the dragon lost the battle and was forced out of heaven. This great dragon – the ancient serpent called the Devil, or Satan, the one deceiving the whole world– was thrown down to the earth with all his angels.

Revelation 12:7-9 NLT

War did not begin on earth or in the physical realm. It began in the unseen realm of the cosmos. War did not start with humans. It is not a product of humanity. Spirits of the dark kingdom influenced humanity to be violent towards each other. There is so much violence recorded in the Bible, I don't understand why the church would mishandle the subject of WAR. The great serpent or dragon originally had the nature of light, worship, and music before the nature of the adversary – "s-a-t-a-n" – [from Hebrew meaning to accuse, obstruct, and oppose} formed in him. The event which created that devilish transformation *may have been* the moment that Lucifer stole the dominion and authority which the Most High God bestowed on Hadam and Havah [Adam and Eve]. After accusing the Most High God of holding back, the "light bringer" convinced the woman Havah to eat and she her husband. Once Hadam ate; the couple was in agreement and the dominion, authority, and *The* blessing came under the accuser's control. According to Isaiah 14:12-14, he attempted to use that "power" which he stole from the first couple to overthrow Almighty Most High God.

Growing up in the church, I heard a myriad of sermons on WAR. Later in my church life, I started hearing Sunday School teachers, preachers, and Bible teachers present lessons on a subject known as spiritual warfare. The prophet Daniel recounts an amazing series of encounters, visions, and relayed stories regarding angels and demons in chapters eight through ten of the Old Testament book which bears his name.

Daniel is informed by a messenger angel of what seems to be an atmospheric conflict above the kingdom of Persia [present day Iran] in which hellish forces delayed the messenger angel in delivering the answer to Daniel's prayers until reinforcement [backup warrior angels] arrived to extricate the messenger from the battle so he could continue to Daniel who was in captivity in Babylon [present day Iraq]. Spiritual warfare? Yes, battles and conflicts in the unseen realm are Biblical truth and yet some who teach on it fail to connect the dots between spiritual warfare and human warfare. We have condemned human warfare as if humans are never influenced, oppressed, and even possessed by unseen personalities which merely ignite a conflict which leads to all out WAR.

The historical accounts of WAR as spelled out in the Bible and film documentaries have resounded in churches for eons and still we haven't connected the dots. The conflicts between humans started as an intended coup against the King of Creation -the Most High God- perpetrated by a lesser "god." (John

14:30/2 Corinthians 4:4)   If the church doesn't get it's theology correct, it will doom it's congregants to being children of the lesser "god." Faith is a matter of eternal life and death to the new creation believer. The New Testament refers to many types of faith including fake and shipwrecked. Think about it. Faith is based on facts as well as life-giving information [from the Latin: to animate].   If we are giving misinformation then the congregants have their faith founded on mis-belief or unbelief [believing wrong]. That makes us vulnerable to the accuser of the Believers.

Under the Old Testament Law, if one kept 99% of it perfectly they were condemned by the holy standards of the righteous Law as being guilty of breaking 100% of it although they only broke 1%. Although we are not under the law but in a covenant of grace (Romans 6:14) which is accessed by faith (Romans 4:16) in *The* Cross, the blood, and the name of Yeshua Jesus; the practice of believing wrong contaminates faith. Could that have a detrimental effect on perfect repentance, authentic contrition, and genuine grace? Think about it.   If we don't agree wholeheartedly where the Word speaks on one issue; could that mean that we are not properly "founded" where we think we completely agree with the Word?

In Exodus 17, Moses' hands were being held up by other men while Joshua fought their enemies in a valley. As long as Moses' shepherd's staff was raised to Heaven, Joshua was victorious. When Moses' arms got heavy and weary and began to drop, the course of the battle would shift towards the enemy's advantage. Once the other two men sat Moshe down and held up his arms for him, Joshua's army fought on to victory. Even with songs about Joshua fighting the battle of Jericho being sung by the children's choirs, the church still didn't have a handle on the necessity of WAR. The media criticizes a political personality over their WAR stances and hypocritically and antagonistically avoids reporting on WAR and oppressive regimes around the world.

If civilized democratic nations heeded the behest of the American entertainment news outlets, the nuclear deterrents would be obliterated, weapons would be destroyed, and the monster rogue nations would swiftly annihilate all who would not bow the knee to the monsters. Sadly, the church is in lock step with the Pharisees of entertainment news rather than the truth of God's Word.

13 You were in Eden, the garden of God; Every precious stone was your covering: The sardius, topaz, and diamond, Beryl, onyx, and jasper, Sapphire, turquoise, and emerald with gold. The workmanship of your timbrels and pipes Was prepared for you on the day you were created.

14 "You were the anointed cherub who covers; I established you; You were on the holy mountain of God; You walked back and forth in the midst of fiery stones.

15 You were perfect in your ways from the day you were created, until iniquity was found in you.

Ezekiel 28:13-15

What was the iniquity or wicked thinking found in Lucifer? The desire to stage a mutiny maybe? Entertaining the idea that he was better and greater than his creator? The Creator? Sounds like celebrity scientists doesn't it?

12 "How you are fallen from heaven, O Lucifer, son of the morning! How you are cut down to the ground, You who weakened the nations!

13 For you have said in your heart: 'I will ascend into heaven, I will exalt my throne above the stars of God; I will also sit on the mount of the congregation On the farthest sides of the north;

14 I will ascend above the heights of the clouds, I will be like the Most High.'

15 Yet you shall be brought down to Sheol, To the lowest depths of the Pit.

16 "Those who see you will gaze at you, And consider you, saying: 'Is this the man who made the earth tremble, Who shook kingdoms,
17 Who made the world as a wilderness And destroyed its cities, Who did not open the house of his prisoners?'   Isaiah 14:12-17

WAR was not implemented by man. WAR started in the unseen realm it seems. WAR started with the Archangel named Lucifer when he decided to overthrow his own Creator. I said, "it seems," in regard to WAR starting in Heaven because it is possible that once the Lucifer antagonist deceived Adam into bowing his knee to the serpent's words and took the authority, dominion, and commanded blessing which the Most High bestowed on humanity; he thought he had enough power to overthrow the Most High Creator God. Can you imagine anything so absurd than the created being turning on the designer who created it?   Well, man has turned on his Creator God. You have turned on your Creator God. I have turned on my Creator God.

All we like sheep have gone astray; we have turned everyone to his own way;   Isaiah 53:6

We all have turned on and away from our Creator God. When Adam fell, there was another WAR which began. The articles of WAR were proclaimed in the judgment which God passed against the serpent. Against the Adversary.

And I will cause hostility between you and the woman, and between your offspring and her offspring. He will strike your head, and you will strike his heel."
Genesis 3:15 NLT

The leader of the kingdom of darkness took humanity hostage and there was no way for the Most High God to rescue the first family without destroying them with His holy nature. Just as a mischievous child looking for mercy after breaking an irreplaceable heirloom, Adam needed the Most High to scoop him up in His arms and say, "It's okay." The problem with that would be the Most High's holy nature would immediately destroy the man because the new sin nature which resulted from the disobedience could not come in contact with pure holiness.

So the Most High kept a SECRET plan close to His "chest". A plan to rescue humanity in a far more exceeding way than anything the kingdom of darkness could ever think or imagine. Pay close attention to the following scriptural excerpts:

And I will put enmity between you and the woman,

And between your seed and her Seed; He shall bruise your head, And you shall bruise His heel."

Genesis 3:15

Now Cain talked with Abel his brother; and it came to pass, when they were in the field, that Cain rose up against Abel his brother and killed him. Genesis 4:8

Right away, the serpent has one brother kill the other in hopes of destroying "The Seed" which Almighty Most High God promised would destroy the serpent. THE FIRST MURDER was over religion. The son which belonged to satan had an insatiable desire to destroy the son which belonged to Almighty Most High God. Your motivations, intentions, and particular reactions will let you know to whom you belong.

2 that the sons of God saw the daughters of men, that they were beautiful; and they took wives for themselves of all whom they chose.
3 And the Lord said, "My Spirit shall not strive with man forever, for he is indeed flesh; yet his days shall be one hundred and twenty years."
4 There were giants on the earth in those days, and also afterward, when the sons of God came in to the daughters of men and they bore children to them. Those were the mighty men who were of old, men of renown.

Genesis 6:2-4

The next attempt was DNA manipulation. Mixing of species to contaminate the blood lines. In 2014, reports were coming out of the scientific community regarding a horrible development. Almighty Most High God created man with a DNA tetragram of four proteins. The horrible development was that biologists supposedly developed two synthetic proteins and introduced them into a substrate containing the four proteins AMHG created and the combination reportedly is compatible. Of course, they think they are potentially curing disease but what they are doing is working on the serpent's secret. He wants a body also.

The earth also was corrupt before God, and the earth was filled with violence. Genesis 6:11

The adversary was intent on destroying "The Seed" even if it meant destroying everyone. Can you guess to whom the violent ones belonged? The power of darkness has been attempting to destroy any seed which belongs to AMHG even to this day. It is interesting that the resolve of those who belong to AMHG only strengthens in face of such threats. God's plan included the use of words to create the body which HE would eventually inhabit. HE gave the words to humans and they spoke them on HIS behalf.

Therefore the Lord Himself will give you a sign: Behold, the virgin shall conceive and bear a Son, and shall call His name Immanuel. [God among us]

Isaiah 7:14

Therefore, when He came into the world, He said: "Sacrifice and offering You did not desire, But a body You have prepared for Me. Hebrews 10:5

A virgin conceiving? Now, that's mind-blowing. How can she conceive and still be called a virgin?

7 But we speak the wisdom of God in a mystery, the hidden wisdom [secret] *which God ordained before the ages for our glory,*
8 which none of the rulers of this age knew; for had they known, they would not have crucified the Lord of glory. 1Corinthians 2:7-8

If the powers of darkness knew what AMHG had planned, they would left "The Seed" alone. What did they find out after the resurrection which gave them pause?

To [HIS chosen] *God willed to make known what are the riches of the glory of this mystery among the Gentiles: which is* CHRIST IN YOU, *the hope of glory.*
Colossians 1:27

Or do you not know that your body is the temple of the Holy Spirit who is in you, whom you have from God, and you are not your own?

1 Corinthians 6:19

Go back to page 62 which references Hebrews were Jesus agrees to inhabit the body which AMHG prepared for HIM. Almighty Most High God wasn't looking for just one body for HIS Son to inhabit but the successful completion of HIS Son's mission in that one body would open up the spirit core of every human who agreed to belong to HIM. Those spirit cores would be inhabited by the Spirit of Almighty Most High God. Can HE keep a secret or what?

Because Lucifer was given (Luke 4:6) the dominion and authority which the Most High gave Adam and Havah [Eve], it probably gave him a bit on insight into the noel – the birth of the Messiah. The birth of Lucifer's destruction. His insight allowed him to preempt the Christmas story by implementing preemptive counterfeits decades and centuries in advance. That is why spiritually dead minds are convinced that pagan stories which predate the noel of Jesus Christ are the real and that the story of Yeshua Messiah is the counterfeit. Highly informed and educated fools have said in their hearts, according to Psalm 53:1, that "there is no God." That statement is referring to the preeminence of the Most High God and Creator of the universe. Not simply that no god at all exists but that THE GOD – CREATOR – who made the smallest nation His prized possession so that He could prove that HE is who HE says HE is. Someone who is touted as one of the most brilliant astrophysical minds said, "The universe created itself because it needed creating." WOW! No fundamental cause and effect from Learning 101? They violate their own foundations to deny the existence of a deliberate, moral, and holy Designer. Spiritually dead human spirits come in all shapes and sizes. Those who ignore the evidence of Almighty Most High God and even deny HIS existence have a rude awakening as the affluent man of Luke chapter six experienced when we woke up in Hell.

If you patiently survey those six scriptural references from the previous five pages or so, you will understand the following narrative. The adversary knew that the *woman's Seed* [JESUS] would crush his head as Almighty Most High God said but he immediately attempted to destroy "The Seed" with the murder of Abel by his brother Cain. After Abel's murder, the enemy attempted to contaminate the human blood line by mixing species. Since the sin nature of the serpent was now the corrupted human nature, the enemy could stop the AMHG's secret and mysterious plans if he could contaminate human DNA and stain bloodlines. The enemy knew that the term *the woman's seed* meant that a body would be prepared for the person who would keep the promise to crush his head.

Violence against women and children was the order of the adversary's day even to this day. The kingdom of darkness was hell bent on destroying the seed before the seed destroyed it. Destroying the woman was an option as well. Violence against women is part and parcel of the WAR the lesser "god" launched against woman's "Seed." The woman is a spiritual nightmare to the kingdom of darkness. She has some special connection/treatment/attention from AMHG. The deceptive workaround is recruiting women as children of the lesser "god" for dark endeavors which promote unimaginable evil. Maybe even convince her to destroy her own seed. Even with the advanced knowledge of the body which Yeshua/Jesus would eventually have, the kingdom of darkness could not stop the strategy.

The mass killing of Hebrew babies in Egypt (Exodus chapters 1 & 2) was part of the continuing campaign the kingdom of darkness launched to destroy "The Seed." The temptations to have the Jews intermarry and mix with the pagan neighbors throughout time was part of the ongoing campaign to destroy "The Seed." Isaiah predicted that a virgin would conceive and give birth to "*God in the flesh*" so the violence against women continued. Still, the kingdom of darkness couldn't stop the AMHG's strategy. Once God was in a body (2 Corinthians 5:19), the kingdom of darkness thought HE was vulnerable enough to kill. Once the kingdom of darkness influenced the religious leaders of Israel to manipulate the Romans into executing the God-Man on a cross, they thought they had finally stopped AMHG's plans to crush the head of the adversary.

The God-Man got up again after being dead for three days. The kingdom of darkness knew they had lost but it wouldn't become abundantly clear to what extent for another nearly fifty days. Jesus visited His followers now and again for nearly forty days before His ascension. He promised to be with His believers forever and to never forsake them and then He was taken away on a cloud. Now that He was gone, the kingdom of darkness thought it was done. Yes, Jesus accomplished His mission and, according to Peter's Day-of-Pentecost sermon, also escaped the "pangs of death" in Hell. Still, He was gone back to Heaven. What did the kingdom of darkness have to fear now.

8 Therefore He says: "When He ascended on high, He

led captivity captive, And gave gifts to men."
9 (Now this, "He ascended" – what does it mean but that He also first descended into the lower parts of the earth?
10 He who descended is also the One who ascended far above all the heavens, that He might fill all things.)   Ephesians 4:8-10 NKJV

And when Jesus returned to Heaven, HE took the group of Old Testament saints from Paradise [also called Abraham's Bosom] with HIM.   Did this protected suburb of Hell rise in the similar what that Atlantis may have fallen?

The Darkness knew that Jesus defeated them but that was just one Jesus. He took His resurrected body and went back to Heaven. But Almighty Most High God still had that SECRET which hadn't been completely unveiled. A secret which surprised the kingdom of darkness to no end. Or rather, to its eventual ending. *The* Cross, blood, and name of Yeshua Jesus made something possible that nobody but the Most High God imagined. On the day of Jesus' crucifixion, the veil in the temple where the presence of Almighty God resided was torn down the middle so the Holy Spirit could get out and relocate. Fifty days later, He took up residence in His new home. On the Day of Pentecost He began taking up residence inside every believer. When Almighty God was planning a body for His Spirit to inhabit, no one knew but Him that He was planning for more than one body to inhabit. On the Day of Pentecost, the kingdom of darkness found out the extent of their loss to Jesus. 120 people inside the Upper Room were now housing the Holy Spirit. Imagine the conversations in the kingdom of darkness. "Wait!" "What?" "What?"

The Darkness influenced the government and religious leaders to kill one Jesus but after Peter preached that Day of Pentecost sermon; three thousand people put faith in *The* Cross, the blood, and the name of Yeshua Jesus and now the God-Man which they killed was inhabiting 3,120 bodies. That is why 1 Corinthians 2:7-8 discloses that if the kingdom of darkness knew that killing one God-Man inhabited body would potentially result in a multitude [of God-Man inhabited bodies] which no man can number (Revelation 7:9) then *"they would not have crucified the Lord of Glory."*

Lucifer initiated WAR in Heaven and the Most High God won the WAR with a decisive victory on *The* Cross and in Hell itself. The spoil of this WAR was one – the soul. Every soul. Jesus freed us from sin according to Romans 6:3-14 just as He declared in His initial sermon in Luke 4:18-19. The redemption of my soul, your soul, and the soul of anyone who will accept it was accomplished by WAR. Even with this glorious development, we still have those who insist on belonging to the spirit of darkness. They use religion, biology, science, and even physics to serve the darkness.

The following scripture passage summarizes the Trump Processional which Yeshua Jesus conducted as He humiliated the monster leaders of the kingdom of darkness and stripped them of their power, authority, and rank.

13 And you, being dead in your trespasses and the uncircumcision of your flesh, He has made alive together with Him, having forgiven you all trespasses,
14 having wiped out the handwriting of requirements that was against us, which was contrary to us. And He has taken it out of the way, having nailed it to the cross.
15 Having disarmed principalities and powers, He made a public spectacle of them, triumphing over them in it.   Colossians 2:13-15

Lucifer initiated WAR in Heaven and Jesus defeated Him in Hell. When HE rose from the dead, HE declared, "*All authority has been given to Me in heaven and on earth.* [because HE took it in the

Trump Processional] *Go therefore and make disciples of all the nations, baptizing them in the name of the Father and of the Son and of the Holy Spirit, teaching them to observe all things that I have commanded you; and lo, I am with you always, even to the end of the age."* (Matthew 28:18-20)

The enemy started the WAR by deceiving the first couple into relinquishing the authority and dominion bestowed on them by AMHG and in doing so enslaved our souls with a sin nature. Jesus went to WAR to free our souls. **He warred in life** by preaching to set minds free and doing miracles to set bodies free. **He warred on** *The* **Cross** to set souls free. **HE warred in the grave and Hell** to free past captives. **HE warred in resurrection** to justify the ungodly and free future captives who put faith in His Cross, blood, and name. And HE was victorious. The WAR was over, the serpent was defeated, and the right to become children of the Most High God was afforded to every human because Jesus' cross, blood, and name saved the eternal day.

For by that one offering he forever made perfect those who are being made holy. Hebrews 10:14

17 Then he says, "I will never again remember their sins and lawless deeds."

18 And when sins have been forgiven, there is no need to offer any more sacrifices. Hebrews 10:17-18

Yes, our Lord and Savior was victorious in rescuing us from our monster captors. The only thing left for us to do is accept it.

Chapter Three

Didn't Jesus Say To Love Everyone?

"You have heard the law that says, 'Love your neighbor' and hate your enemy.   But I say, love your enemies! Pray for those who persecute you!

Matthew 5:43-44

The most common mistake church people make is applying Jesus' teachings on interpersonal relationships to the relationships between nation states and to those between the law and law breakers. The governments of the nation states are tasked with keeping their populace safe as well as providing for the common defense and ensure domestic tranquility as well. "Capital punishment must be abolished," some people say, "because Jesus said to love everybody." Such misguided theology is extremely dangerous.

There are some people in the world who no matter how many times they hear the message of the transforming grace of Almighty Most High God will not submit to the Lordship of Jesus and repent of their sins. The two men crucified beside Jesus which were called "malefactors" by the King James Bible were criminals for whom rehabilitation would not work. The repentant criminal wasn't rehabilitated by the Roman flagrum or the hard labor. He was transformed, however, by what he witnessed as Jesus was dying in the same way he was. Jesus did curse back at the mockers who cursed HIM and the other two crucified ones. Instead, HE prayed for them, asked HIS Father to forgive them, and quoted scripture the whole time. Maybe the repentant criminal recognized some of the quotes.

The Romans did make statements to the populace at large when crucifying criminals but they preferred to turn them into a labor force instead. Those who ended up being crucified were the ones which would not be what the military force wanted them to be.

As we survey the scriptures we will find that relationship dynamics are dealt with on multiple levels. Personal relationships are the ones which individuals are responsible for. Whether family, workplace, or social; the personal relationships are the ones our Savior commented on the most. Even the soldiers inquired of *John the Baptiser* regarding proper repentance and he instructed them regarding their interactions with the population at large as well as with their employer.

"You have heard the law that says, 'Love your neighbor' and hate your enemy.
44 But I say, love your enemies! Pray for those who persecute you!
45 In that way, you will be acting as true children of your Father in heaven. For he gives his sunlight to both the evil and the good, and he sends rain on the just and the unjust alike.
46 If you love only those who love you, what reward is there for that? Even corrupt tax collectors do that much.

47 If you are kind only to your friends, how are you different from anyone else? Even pagans do that.
48 But you are to be perfect, even as your Father in heaven is perfect.   Matthew 5:43-48 NLT

3 For the authorities do not strike fear in people who are doing right, but in those who are doing wrong. Would you like to live without fear of the authorities? Do what is right, and they will honor you.
4 The authorities are God's servants, sent for your good. But if you are doing wrong, of course you should be afraid, for they have the power to punish you. THEY ARE GOD'S SERVANTS, *sent for the very purpose of punishing those who do what is wrong.*
                    Romans 13:3-4 NLT

The agents of the state and government – law enforcement and military – are servants of God. For some reason, the church has made the mistake of equating Jesus' teachings on interpersonal relationships with what the Word teaches regarding the relationship between foreign states, governments, and imperially aggressive nations. Jesus' teachings regarding forgiveness and love pertain to interpersonal relationships. State, governments, and nations cannot forgive because forgiveness comes from an individual's heart, mind, and motivations. Enforcing the law should be exacting but because of the human factor it cannot be. The demanding requirements of "fixing" a wrong after the law has been "broken" involve justice. At the same time, the human factor interjects mercy and mitigation if deemed warranted. Still, the ecclesiastical arenas are not steadfast on what the Word of God teaches on socially incendiary issues.

We teach and preach against WAR because we should "love one another." Some think it is Biblical to hold such a view but is it? In the same regard, I have heard church people condemn the death penalty because, "we are supposed to love one another." Individuals don't carry out capital punishment. Not legally at least. States, governments, and courts do in the course of enforcing laws. The consequences for violating the laws are clear.

THE WORD DOES NOT command governments and nation states to love everybody. It instructs God's people to love everybody. NOT EVERYONE belongs to God according to

Genesis
Exodus 7
Joshua
Judges
Psalms

Jeremiah 12
Matthew 13
Matthew 23
2 Corinthians 6
Revelation

The only government entity instructed to extend love is church government. The authority of church government applies to confessing believers who defiantly continue in known sin. Church government is even entrusted with enforcement of the spiritual "laws" of Christian conduct and societal and communal behavior but it is also instructed to extend mercy, grace, and reconciliation IF IF IF genuine contrition and authentic repentance are voiced and displayed. (1 Corinthians 5:1-13/ 2 Corinthians 2:1-13/James 5:19-20) Jesus criticized the religious leadership in Matthew 23:23 for doling out judgment without allowing for mercy and justice. Church government is expected to be merciful and gracious if proper response and repentance precede it. Secular government is expected to protect and serve its populace and push back against invading threats.

The good news about the book of Revelation is that it tells of peoples who belong or belonged to the Almighty but either lost their way, their perspective, their affection, their purpose or their "first love."

What's good about the way John the Revelator pens these visions and mysteries is it shows that God's people can find their way back to HIM. HE will honor free will and pro choice to the very end. If you choose to do things your way instead of AMHG's then you will get your reward instead of HIS. (Revelation 22:12)

Throughout the Old Testament you see the designation *the children of Israel* [Jacob/God's Prince]. When the "*heel catcher's*" name was changed in Genesis 32 from Jacob to Israel, a new revelation of God's grace was unveiled. In the language of types and shadows, who is ultimately the Almighty's Prince but Yeshua Jesus?

When you take a close look at Jesus' teaching on love in the sixth chapter of Luke's gospel, I challenge you to apply those admonitions to nation states, aggressive communist armies, and even to the jurist imprudence of activist judges in courts of law. No, love doesn't come from a government. Forgiveness isn't inherent in a nation state. Those attributes are dimensions of soul, emotion, and intent.

35 But love your enemies, do good, and lend, hoping for nothing in return; and your reward will be great, and you will be sons of the Most High. For He is kind

to the unthankful and evil.
36 Therefore be merciful, just as your Father also is
merciful.   Luke 6:35-36

Can a nation state be a child of my Most High Father?   Only symbolically unless HE says differently. But you can as an individual IF you love HIS way and not the world's way.   The world's system says that, "love is love is love is love," BUT THAT IS NOT WHAT THE BIBLE TEACHES.   In the Greek language alone, there are several words which are translated love.   At least four of them are used in the New Testament.

Eros	Physical, erotic, and superficial love
Philia	Deep friendship or brotherly love
Ludus	Playful, naïve or "puppy love"
Agape	Unconditional love or grace
Pragma	Longstanding love (Marriage)
Philautia	Strong self image
Stergo	Parental love

In the Old Testament, several words for love are used in the Hebrew language.

Ahava	Spontaneous
Hesed	Deliberate affection or covenant love
Raham	Devotional love from a caregiver to a

	family member or patient
Yada	Intimate sexual knowledge
	ALSO used in the word praise
Shahaq	Playful love
Dawad	Caressing love

Of course, this is a rather elementary display of these words but the point is crystal clear that love is not love is not love. Words actually mean something in Heaven and earth. In the unseen realm as well in this physical realm. Maybe we should attend to the way the Creator of Words uses words. According to the Word of the Living God, the Almighty is love. Look at 1st John 4:8:

*He who does not love does not know God [the Supreme Divinity], for **the Supreme Divinity** is love.*
*And we have come to know and have believed the love which God has for us. **God is love**, and the one who abides in love abides in God, and God abides in him.* 1John 4:16 NASB

9 In this the love of God was manifested toward us, that God has sent His only begotten Son into the world, that we might live through Him.
10 In this is love, not that we loved God, but that He loved us and sent His Son to be the propitiation for our sins. 1 John 4:9-10

So, IF YOUR LOVE DOESN'T mirror the love of Almighty Most High God, you definitely need to reassess.

Here is an excellent display of the *Supreme Divinity's* love for humanity. He loved us too much to leave us the way we were. Now, that's Love. Real Love. HE loves you enough to let you have your way even if it is not the best way for you. HE will honor your choice to reject HIS gift of eternal life and HIS rescue of you from eternal death.

He went to WAR with the bully which took the souls of humanity hostage and enslaved them using his devilish sin nature. And because of *The* Cross, the blood, and the name of Messiah Yeshua the doors of our prison cells have been torn apart and we have been set free. Now, if we refuse to accept Jesus' cross, blood, and name as the Word of the Most High God has presented to us then we choose to remain in cells which we can easily walk out. By simply saying, "YES!" to the liberating force of Heaven and walking free out of those prison cells of our minds, ignorance, racism, religion, humanism, secularism, and false humility.

After the fall, every human except Jesus was born spiritually dead and enslaved by sin. Because of His cross, blood, name, and resurrection, we can be born again – born free – born from above – IF, IF, IF we simply accept this matchless gift (2ⁿᵈ Corinthians 9:15) with simply saying from the bottom of our hearts,

"Yes Jesus, Yes!"

20 For all of God's promises have been fulfilled in Christ with a resounding "Yes!" And through Christ, our "Amen" (which means "Yes") ascends to God for his glory.
21 It is God who enables us, along with you, to stand firm for Christ. He has commissioned us,
22 and he has identified us as his own by placing the Holy Spirit in our hearts as the first installment that guarantees everything he has promised us.

2 Corinthians 1:20-22 NLT

Yes Jesus, Yes!

Gerald McCray

Chapter Four

JEHOVAH, "Man" Of WAR?

The LORD is a Man of War; The Lord is His name. Pharaoh's chariots and his army He has cast into the sea; His chosen captains also are drowned in the Red Sea.

Exodus 15:3-4 NKJV

In the 14ᵗʰ chapter of Exodus, the people of Israel are promised that, "The Lord shall fight for you," as the Egyptian army was barreling down on them from behind and the impossible Red Sea was facing them. It turned out that they did not have to fight at all. The scriptural theme for this chapter from the 15ᵗʰ chapter of Exodus is a reference to how the former nation of Egyptian slaves rejoiced when their previous captors were drowned in the sea while attempting to retrieve them and return them to slavery.   The economy of Egypt collapsed gradually over a series of wonders and marvels which the Most High God performed in Egypt and the slave enclave of Goshen simultaneously.   When Egypt was being bombarded with plagues, the chosen people of the Most High God were being protected and even flourishing.   The final plague from the original universe of marvels broke the camel's back and Egypt's economy.   When the Egyptians attempted to retrieve God's first born and return them to slavery, the military might of Egypt was broken.

The Lord will fight for you, and you shall hold your peace."   Exodus 14:14

When the emancipated slaves were traveling from Egypt towards the land which the Most High God and Creator of land deeded to Avraham, the Egyptian army came in heavy pursuit to reclaim the Hebrew Israelites. The sea was ahead of them and the Egyptian army was hot on their heels. They saw no way out of that dilemma. While the people panicked Moses was praying [listening to the LORD]. Moses told the people that that they should calm down and kept their peace because the Most High God would deal with their enemy on His terms. Why?

If you go back to the fourth chapter of Exodus when the Most High God spoke to Moses out of the burning bush, you will hear something rather interesting.

Then you shall say to Pharaoh, 'Thus says the Lord: "Israel is My son, My firstborn..."   Exodus 4:22

The Creator of Heaven and Earth called this nation of slaves not only His offspring but something much much more. His firstborn son. If you study it out you will find that the firstborn has huge significance in the Hebrew culture. The sacrifices had to be the first. The tithes offered to the LORD had to be the first of the revenue or crops and not just leftovers. The first portion sanctified or guaranteed blessings on the rest. The firstborn was a significant term to the Egyptians as well. The Egyptian men and especially the Pharaohs believed that their security and status in the afterlife was directly linked to birth and lives of their firstborn males. Pharaoh understood exactly what was being relayed to him when Moses' mouth piece voiced those words to Pharaoh. Still, his hard heart resisted the instruction of the Most High God and it took all of the plagues to happen before Ramses agreed to release the Hebrews.

So, ABBA Father (Matthew14:36/Romans 8:15/Galatians 4:6), the God-Man of WAR fought for His children. His firstborn. Take a look at some scriptures regarding His determination to protect and even redeem His children through WAR:

7 Open up, O ancient gates, and let the King of Glory in.
8 Who is this King of Glory? **The Lord, strong and mighty, invincible in battle.**
9 Yes, open wide the gates and let the King of Glory in.
10 Who is this King of Glory? The Commander of all of heaven's armies! Psalms 24:7-10 TLB

14 Then the Lord said to Moses, "Write this for a memorial in the book and recount it in the hearing of Joshua, that I will utterly blot out the remembrance of Amalek from under heaven."
15 And Moses built an altar and called its name,

The-Lord-Is-My-Banner; [Jehovah-Nissi]
16 for he said, "Because the Lord has sworn: the Lord will have WAR with Amalek from generation to generation."   Exodus 17:14-16

Amalek was a descendent of Esau whose hatred of his brother Jacob [renamed Israel in Genesis 32:28] has lasted to this day. The hatred of Ismail [Islam?] towards his half brother Isaac [the father of Jacob-Israel] has lasted to this day. The hatred of Agar [mother of Ismail] towards Abraham and Sarah [grandmother of Israel] has lasted to this day. I don't know if you have ever connected the dots but the Bible seems to teach that hatred can be hereditary. It can be passed down to future generations along with genetic traits.

3 So Moses spoke to the people, "Equip some of your men for WAR. They will go against Midian to inflict the Lord's vengeance on them.
4 Send 1,000 men to war from each Israelite tribe."
5 So 1,000 were recruited from each Israelite tribe out of the thousands in Israel–12,000 equipped for war.
6 Moses sent 1,000 from each tribe to war. They went with Phinehas son of Eleazar the priest, in whose care were the holy objects and signal trumpets.
                    Numbers 31:3-6 ASB

[YAHWEH] trains my hands for war; my arms can bend a bow of bronze. Psalms 18:34 ASB

9 Then I went to the governors in the region beyond the River, and gave them the king's letters. Now the king had sent captains of the army and horsemen with me.
10 When Sanballat the Horonite and Tobiah the Ammonite official heard of it, they were deeply disturbed that a man had come to seek the well-being of the children of Israel. Nehemiah 2:9-10

19 But when Sanballat the Horonite, Tobiah the Ammonite [incestal descendant of Lot] official, and Geshem the Arab heard of it, they laughed at us and despised us, and said, "What is this thing that you are doing? Will you rebel against the king?"
20 So I answered them, and said to them, "The God of heaven Himself will prosper us; therefore we His servants will arise and build, but you have no heritage or right or memorial in Jerusalem."

Nehemiah 2:19-20

The children of Ba'al/Ballat/Allat/Alla along with some Arab descendants of Ismail and Ammonite descendants of Esau conspired to destroy the Jews who were rebuilding the dilapidated walls of Jerusalem. Nehemiah got permission from his captives to leave captivity to return to Jerusalem to raise the ruins.   Nehemiah even had a military security detail assigned to him as he went to survey the ruins.   Sanballat [maybe "son" of Allat] was a Persian [Iran] political leader and public official.   His close assistant was Tobiah who was an Ammonite descendant of Esau.   Ammonites were distant Semitic relatives of the Hebrews but were pagan worshippers of Molech/Moloch [from Horus worship in Egypt?] where children were thrown into the statue's fire or laid upon its heated arms and cooked to death. Whole nations were killing their own "Seed" rather than protect and cherish it.   Any wonder why Most High God wanted to clean out the land?   What will happen to a nation like America which has killed maybe seventy five million babies inside the womb? God only knows.

7 Now it happened, when Sanballat, Tobiah, the Arabs, the Ammonites, and the Ashdodites heard that the walls of Jerusalem were being restored and the gaps were beginning to be closed, that they became very angry,
8 and all of them conspired together to come and attack Jerusalem and create confusion.

Nehemiah 4:7-8

These Moslem, Arab, Palestinian, and Idumean [Esau]

ancestors of Hebrew/Israelite haters heard that the ruins were being rebuilt and agreed to just go to Jerusalem to kill all of those involved in the rebuilding project. To whom to do supposed they belonged? The Spirit of Almighty Most High God or the spirit of darkness? Nehemiah wasn't looking for WAR but he was prepared for it. He wasn't on the offensive but was ready at a moment's notice to defend the "City of Peace -Jerusalem.

15 When our enemies heard that we were aware of their plot and that God had frustrated it, we all returned to the wall, each to his own work.
16 From that day on, half of my men did the work, while the other half were equipped with spears, shields, bows and armor. The officers posted themselves behind all the people of Judah
17 who were building the wall. Those who carried materials did their work with one hand and held a weapon in the other,
18 and each of the builders wore his sword at his side as he worked. But the man who sounded the trumpet stayed with me. Nehemiah 4:15-18 NIV

Being ready and resolved to finish a WAR and being aggressively intent on world domination are two diametrically opposed positions. One nation threatens WAR and another responds with equally opposite rhetoric and both leaders are put into the same category. How screwed up is that? The church for some reason doesn't know the difference. Israel was in danger of constant threats from aggressive nations simply because they were favored as the precious treasure (Exodus 19:5) of Almighty Most High God – Creator of Heaven and earth. Pagan nations of the world have harbored vitriol towards the Most High's prized possession for centuries simply to disprove that Jews are the chosen people of Almighty God.

Those promises by the Most High God to the patriarchs and the nation of the Hebrews/Israelites have been in holy writ for eons. The distinction the LORD makes between this "smallest" nation which HE decided to use to prove His existence and the multitude of anti-Bible pagan nations is the cause of the vitriol. The destruction of the Jews/Hebrews/Israelites/Israel has been the desire and strategy of their enemy nations to disprove the promises of the Pentateuch, Torah, and Old Testament prophesies. Destroying Israel and the Jews would, in essence, disprove the holy scriptures. Bible Study Teacher Les Feldick said it best with, "*The Jew makes the Bible true.*" As target of the majority of the world's nations, Israel still is instructed to love. Still, that love doesn't mean to trust the enemy or lay down the defensive weapons.

One day the nations of the world will bring all of their wealth and resources to bear in siege of Israel and the fight for the city of peace will near the final solution in the valley of decision.   Jehovah's decision.

13 It shall come to pass in that day that a great panic from the Lord will be among them. Everyone will seize the hand of his neighbor, And raise his hand against his neighbor's hand;
14 Judah also will fight at Jerusalem. And the wealth of all the surrounding nations Shall be gathered together: Gold, silver, and apparel in great abundance.
Zechariah 14:13-14

The antagonist nations of the world will one day besiege Jerusalem and threaten its existence.   They will think that it is the last time Israel will be a going concern. They will be fatally mistaken. The LORD of Creation will interrupt this WAR and rescue His firstborn nation. The Ancient of Days will unleash the Hosts of Heaven to put an end to this aggression.

And it will be glorious!

Chapter Five

The Armor? Of God?

Therefore take up the whole armor of God, that you may be able to withstand in the evil day, and having done all, to stand. Stand therefore

Ephesians 6:13-14a NKJV

Why do you think Almighty Most High God has made HIS armor available to HIS children? Shouldn't the mention of HIS armor cause us to reevaluate our mindset on WAR? Or should we simply ignore the warnings of us having a constant threat against us by a committed adversary? (1st Peter 5:8) Connect the dots.

ALSO, this scripture says, "whole armor" for some specific reason. Is it possible that some believers were not accepting the entire message of *The* Cross? Salvation was easily accepted because the dying Jesus did on HIS cross was obvious but what about justification? What about righteousness? Was it difficult for new believers to accept the fact that faith in Jesus' blood made them INSTANEOUSLY righteous? Two thousand years of Bible teaching and today's church has the same obstacles.

This "armor of God" scripture harkens back to the *War In Heaven?* chapter of this book. WAR started in the unseen realm. The full detailed description of this armor in the sixth chapter of Ephesians clearly correlates the natural pieces of armor with a spiritual reality. Believers and receivers of *The* Cross, the blood, and the name of Jesus Christ can find their spiritual identity in the spiritual armor of Almighty God. Amazingly, the armor of Most High God is permanently bequeathed to those who become HIS children. The moment the ungodly put faith in The Cross, the blood, and the name (Romans 4:5) of Yeshua Jesus, they instantly are fitted for the armor. Immediately, they can take possession of the best spiritual protection the universe has ever known.

What is absolutely intriguing is the specificity of the military symbolism with which Paul compares the Roman soldier's protective gear with the spiritual garb which YAHWEH'S grace offers to dress the soldiers of *The* Cross. Rick Renner's book *Dressed To Kill* is a scriptural schematic on the spiritual protection which Jesus' cross, blood, and name have established for every believer IF they believe it. I have yet to read Renner's book but have had the pleasure of watching his lectures on the armor of God via the Believer's Voice Of Victory Network. Truly a spiritual jolt of faith and confidence. Look at Ephesians 6:10-20 here:

10 Finally, my brethren, be strong in the Lord and in the power of His might. [His might not ours]
11 Put on the whole armor of God, that you may be able to stand against the wiles of the devil.
12 For we do not wrestle against flesh and blood, but against principalities, against powers, against the rulers of the darkness of this age, against spiritual hosts of

wickedness in the heavenly places.
13 Therefore take up the whole armor of God, that you may be able to withstand in the evil day, and having done all, to stand.
14 Stand therefore, having girded your waist with truth, having put on the breastplate of righteousness,
15 and having shod your feet with the preparation of the gospel of peace;
16 above all, taking the shield of faith with which you will be able to quench all the fiery darts of the wicked one.
17 And take the helmet of salvation, and the sword of the Spirit, which is the Word of God;
18 praying always with all prayer and supplication in the Spirit, being watchful to this end with all perseverance and supplication for all the saints –
19 and for me, that utterance may be given to me, that I may open my mouth boldly to make known the mystery of the gospel,
20 for which I am an ambassador in chains; that in it I may speak boldly, as I ought to speak.

girdle	truth
breastplate	righteousness,
hobnailed boots	the gospel of peace
shield	faith to quench fiery darts
helmet	salvation – Yeshua Jesus
sword	Spirit/the word of YAHWEH

Along with the backpack of supplies which a Roman soldier carried, nearly 140 pounds were added to their bodies. The armor of the Almighty God adds weight and gravity to our spiritual identities. Just as the natural armor makes the soldier heftier, the armor of Almighty God makes us spiritually sturdy and robust. The terms anointing and glory carry the connotation of weightiness, gravity, and importance. Gravitas? Robust righteousness? Sturdy embracing truth? Strapping peace? Wow!

The wiles of the enemy are many. Just as conventional human conflict involves stealth tactics, so do the strategies of the kingdom of darkness. The reference to Most High God preparing a body for His presence to inhabit for the redemption of humanity, the wicked one has devised a plan to inhabit a body for the intended deception and destruction of as many souls as he can. The original tactics included influence, manipulation, cerebral coercion, and possession to get his dark agents to kill, abuse, break, oppress, enslave, etc.

Fight the good fight of faith, lay hold on eternal life, to which you were also called and have confessed the good confession in the presence of many witnesses.
1 Timothy 6:12

6 For I am already being poured out as a drink offering, and the time of my departure is at hand.
7 I have fought the good fight, I have finished the race, I have kept the faith.
8 Finally, there is laid up for me the crown of righteousness, which the Lord, the righteous Judge, will give to me on that Day, and not to me only but also to all who have loved His appearing.

2 Timothy 4:6-8

The armor of God properly equips us to fight the good fight. We at times fight for faith. At other times, we fight or wrestle with faith. Faith is contrary to our natural minds and contradicts natural and common sense. An excellent Bible Study teacher once said that the Word of Almighty God wasn't given to men to make sense but to make faith. (Copeland) It is the revelation of the armor of God which helps us to side with faith and obliterate the wiles of the enemy.

The armor of Almighty Most High God protects our **righteousness.** The armor of Almighty Most High God establishes us in the covenant of grace with truth, the whole **truth,** and nothing but the truth. The armor of Almighty Most High God grounds us in a relationship of **peace** with Him. Peace that makes no sense at all. Peace which surpasses any human or demonic comprehension. The armor of Almighty

Most High God protects us with a full body shield of faith. The armor of Almighty Most High God protects our minds, emotions, souls, and spiritual cognition from "head" wounds with a **salvation** or rescue **helmet.** Since Jesus' Hebrew name Yeshua/Yehoshua means rescue or salvation AND because HE is the Head of HIS body [the church], guess what [OR WHO] the helmet of salvation is made of? (1st Corinthians 2:16) Although a shield can be used as a bludgeoning weapon, the only specifically offensive weapon which is named in the list of armor is the **sword** of the Spirit which is also called *The* Word of God. Think about it. How do we understand the Almighty's promises and realities of justification, sanctification, truth, righteousness, the gospel, peace, faith, and salvation?

It is through HIS Word isn't it? The Sword of The Spirit is the most important piece of the uniform because it helps us understand how *The* Cross, the blood, and the name of Yeshua Jesus has established our spiritual identities once and for all [Hebrews 10:10] into this covenant of grace (Romans 5:2) in which we find ourselves. A spiritual identity which clearly states in Ephesians 4:24 that our new creation spirit core is made out of the "God stuff" in *righteousness and true holiness.* This covenant of grace is expected to unfold for eons and ages to come according to Ephesians 2:7. Thousands of years from now we will still be learning about what makes the grace covenant so amazing.

When Paul was correlating the different pieces of the soldier's uniform to the concepts of the faith, his Ephesus audience had a mental picture of the soldiers and could, in faith, place those pieces of armor on themselves. The different pieces of armor mean nothing to the novice or even the religiously minded person. The imagery does mean everything to anyone who has an elementary understanding of the faith. Justification, salvation, gospel, peace, truth, and righteousness can all be better understood by this imagery.

What the imagery also does is motivate the believer to learn as much as possible about the different realities of salvation, grace, and *The* Cross. When the listeners of the Ephesus letter saw a Roman soldier after hearing this imagery they had their faith strengthened in the fact that Almighty God's spiritual armor is even more real than the soldier's uniform they were viewing in the moment.

YOU WARRIORS WITH WOUNDED SOULS and tortured minds cannot find deep spiritual healing from superficial treatments. Only Almighty Most

High God can heal the wounded soul. Only HIS Word can perform the necessary repairs on your minds. You will never forget but you can find peace once you give it all to Him never to pick it up again after He throws it into His sea of forgetfulness and forgiveness. (Micah 7:19)

Some people may attempt to coach you into forgetting the atrocities which haunt you. That is impossible. Some erroneously teach that the Word of God instructs us to forgive and forget. That is inaccurate. The Word teaches us that God Himself can forgive and forget but that is God. He has the unique ability to forget or never associate you with whatever you repented of. (Psalm 103:12) You will be instructed and coached to forgive yourself and rightly so but YOU CANNOT FORGIVE YOURSELF DEFINITIVELY UNLESS YOU KNOW FOR SURE THAT YOUR HEAVENLY FATHER HAS FORGIVEN YOU. And once you know for sure that you have been forgiven, then you can finally forgive yourself and live.

The Cross, the blood, and the name of Jesus covers it all. You have to put it all at the foot of Jesus' cross along with the sins of the past as well as the sin condition we all find ourselves in. Yes, He wants to heal everything which oppresses you according to Acts 10:38 but you must cooperate with Him. The majority of the miraculous face to face encounters which we read about in the gospels which people had with Jesus were not pleas for eternal salvation but for temporal relief of a malady or spiritual oppression. **Jesus heals unsaved people.** Jesus heals saved people. Jesus heals those who ask HIM to. Jesus heals those who believe HE can and will. Still, the main reason HE came was to save all of us from God's judgment against the sin condition and sinful acts. You can put it all at the foot of His cross right now. Use your own words or these from Romans 10:6-12:

6 But faith's way of getting right with God says, "Don't say in your heart, 'Who will go up to heaven' (to bring Christ down to earth).
7 And don't say, 'Who will go down to the place of the dead' (to bring Christ back to life again)."
8 In fact, it says, "The message is very close at hand; it is on your lips and in your heart." And that message is the very message about faith that we preach:
9 <u>If you confess with your mouth that Jesus is Lord and believe in your heart that God raised him from the dead,</u> you will be saved.
10 For it is by believing in your heart that you are made right with God, and it is by confessing with your mouth that you are saved.
11 As the Scriptures tell us, "ANYONE WHO TRUSTS IN HIM WILL NEVER BE DISGRACED."

12 Jew and Gentile are the same in this respect. They have the same Lord, who gives generously to all who call on him.   Romans 10:6-12 NLT

"Anyone who trusts HIM will NEVER be separated from grace" is an exciting promise.   The Word of Almighty God coming out of our mouths can dress us in the armor of God. We put it on by faith. We already have it given to us by *The* Cross but it is good practice to speak it and take it up and put it on daily. The Word of God coming out of our mouths can get us right with Almighty Most High God. Once you understand what the Word says, you can do it with simply, "Yes Jesus, Yes!"

Chapter Six

The WAR Within

For I delight in the law of God according to the inward man.   But I see another law in my members, warring against the law of my mind, and bringing me into captivity to the law of sin which is in my members.   O wretched man that I am! Who will deliver me from this body of death?

Romans 7:22-24

Apostle Paul goes into a point and counter point soliloquy regarding the attempt to work for righteousness versus receiving Jesus' imputed righteousness afforded by faith in HIS cross, blood, and name. How does this relate to the wounded soul? Regret, guilt, and self condemnation can have us working in some way or the other to make up for the wrong we've done. We never can work enough to make up for our sins or work enough to satisfy our sin debt or soothe our consciences. The sixth chapter of Hebrews calls that type of activity "*dead works.*"

It is this internal conflict which the wounded soul must endure the most. Realizing that we cannot do anything to make up for the past results is desperation, hopelessness, and self destructive thinking. We can't work enough to make up for our sins but we can surrender to the One who can make us new on the inside like sin never happened.

On a bit of a similar note, the couple which has agreed to terminate their baby in the womb out of convenience may find themselves engaged in some futile attempt to make up for it by adopting a small army of "rescue babies" in some effort to ease their consciences or abate their guilt and regret. Somehow making it up to the aborted ones by completely devoting themselves to the current ones. Taking care of rescue babies is absolutely amazing and a definite necessity. I just want to be clear that you cannot work enough to make up for the sins of the past. That has already been done by Jesus on *The* Cross. Yes, continue to rescue the babies. Just be careful not to put yourselves on the hamster wheel of condemnation trying to make up for something you can never make up for. Just repent to God, ask for forgiveness, and lay it at the foot of *The* Cross.

10 Create in me a clean heart, O God, And renew a steadfast spirit within me.
11 Do not cast me away from Your presence, And do not take Your Holy Spirit from me.
12 Restore to me the joy of Your salvation, And uphold me by Your generous Spirit.

Psalms 51:10-12

You followed orders and hurt people. You followed orders and others lost their lives. You followed orders and the damage you left in your wake is tearing you apart. Some of the damage you left in your wake had nothing to do with orders. You cannot seem to reconcile what you know about being good or righteous with the actions you took and the collateral damage you left behind. If conscientious warriors cannot reconcile these dilemmas they may find themselves at a crossroad in which they entertain the idea of hurting themselves as a sort of penance or personal reparation towards those they damaged. Maybe some may think that they have gone much too far for God's amazing grace to reach them.

Well, you don't have to do penance. Jesus already completed your penance for you on *The* Cross. You don't have to offer reparations in order to find peace with Almighty Most High God. HE has already resolved the situation for you and dealt with the consequences on your behalf. *The* Cross of Jesus is where Most High God laid on Jesus the punishment for ALL of our sins (Isaiah 53:6) and because Jesus successfully accomplished His mission, we who put faith in His cross, His blood, and His name have been justified by Jesus' sacrifice (Isaiah 53:11) which resulted in ALL OF US being able to accept His taking away ALL OF OUR sins because He indentified with us transgressors, sinners, and wicked.

9 But those who desire to be rich fall into temptation and a snare, *and into many foolish and harmful lusts* which drown men in destruction *and perdition.*
10 For the love of money is a root of all kinds of evil, for which some have strayed from the faith in their greediness, and pierced themselves through with many sorrows.
11 But you, O man of God, flee these things and

pursue righteousness, godliness, faith, love, patience, gentleness.

12 Fight the good fight of faith, *lay hold on eternal life, to which you were also called and have confessed the good confession in the presence of many witnesses.*   1 Timothy 6:9-12

The inner battle can arise from the desire of the flesh to work for something which it can never earn — grace. The sixth chapter of Hebrews calls religious activity which harbors the motivation of working and clawing its way into Heaven simply DEAD WORKS (Hebrews 6:1). Isaiah 54:6 says that a life completely devoted to doing righteousness for the purpose of earning peace with God adds up to nothing but a pile of filthy rags soiled by a bloody discharge. **If we could work enough to earn grace** then it would no longer be grace but wages for services rendered according to Romans 4:4. If we put faith in the work which Almighty Most High God did through Jesus to make us right with Him through His work and none of ours; Romans 4:5 tells us that we are justified by Almighty God Himself. He did that long before you did what you did.

14 For we know that the law is spiritual, but I am carnal, sold under sin.

15 For what I am doing, I do not understand. For

what I will to do, that I do not practice; but what I hate, that I do.

16 If, then, I do what I will not to do, I agree with the law that it is good.

17 But now, it is no longer I who do it, but sin that dwells in me.

18 For I know that in me (that is, in my flesh) nothing good dwells; for to will is present with me, but how to perform what is good I do not find.

19 For the good that I will to do, I do not do; but the evil I will not to do, that I practice.

20 Now if I do what I will not to do, it is no longer I who do it, but sin that dwells in me.

21 I find then a law, that evil is present with me, the one who wills to do good.

22 For I delight in the law of God according to the inward man.

23 But I see another law in my members, warring against the law of my mind, and bringing me into captivity to the law of sin which is in my members.

24 O wretched man that I am! Who will deliver me from this body of death?

25 I thank God – through Jesus Christ our Lord! So then, with the mind I myself serve the law of God, but with the flesh the law of sin.   Romans 7:14-25

Verse 24 is telling us that trying to work for grace is like dragging a corpse around on our backs. Busy religious work either in the church or in the community is a no win situation. So, how do we get there when we can't do it on our own? Surrendering to Jesus to allow Him to do the work which no one else can will result in us being made what we were originally supposed to be.

16 So I say, let the Holy Spirit guide your lives. Then you won't be doing what your sinful nature craves.
17 The sinful nature wants to do evil, which is just the opposite of what the Spirit wants. And the Spirit gives us desires that are the opposite of what the sinful nature desires. These two forces are constantly fighting each other, so you are not free to carry out your good intentions.
18 But when you are directed by the Spirit, you are not under obligation to the law of Moses.
Galatians 5:16-18 NLT

3 He restores my soul; He leads me in the paths of righteousness For His name's sake.
4 Yea, though I walk through the valley of the shadow of death, I will fear no evil; For You are with me; Your rod and Your staff, they comfort me.   Psalms 23:3-4

but there is something else deep within me, in my lower nature, that is at WAR with my mind and wins the fight and makes me a slave to the sin that is still within me. In my mind I want to be God's willing servant, but instead I find myself still enslaved to sin. So you see how it is: my new life tells me to do right, but the old nature that is still inside me loves to sin. Oh, what a terrible predicament I'm in! Who will free me from my slavery to this deadly lower nature? Thank God! It has been done by Jesus Christ our Lord. He has set me free. Romans 7:23-25 TLB

Attempting to work for grace is the same as being enslaved to sin. There is no hope for us to free ourselves from sin. The great news is that Jesus already did all the heavy lifting to free us from sin. We only need to accept His free gift of gracious love and salvation.

Many years ago, I had a Bible lexicon which defined the word "confess" as regurgitation. When we tell Almighty Most High God what He already knows, it has the benefit of purging our souls, minds, and spirits of the sins, wounds, regret, guilt, and condemnation which stalk us and threaten our peace.

Confess your trespasses to one another, and pray for one another, that you may be healed. The effective, fervent prayer of a righteous man avails much.

James 5:16

Confessing is cleansing. Confessing is an extremely important and critical step to finally being free. Confessing purges the soul. Confessing cleanses the sprit. Confessing which is shored up by the grace of *The* Cross heals the wounded heart, soul, mind, and emotions.

Gerald McCray

Chapter Seven

We

Are

Redeemed!

*Having disarmed principalities and powers, He made a
public spectacle of them, triumphing over them in it.*
Colossians 2:15 NKJV

Yes we are redeemed by the sacrifices of WAR. Jesus' blood was shed in combat to redeem and resurrect our dead spirit cores. Jesus fought by staying on *The Cross* in excruciating pain and anguish rather than save Himself from the suffering. War liberated Nazi occupied Europe. War liberated Nazi bombarded Britain. War liberated our sin, death, and darkness occupied souls. Jesus defeated the kingdom of darkness on its turf and then paraded them in humiliation while our spirits and souls were put in the perfect position to celebrate victory.

The Trump Processional

11 In Him you were also circumcised with the circumcision made without hands, by putting off the body of the sins of the flesh, by the circumcision of Christ,
12 buried with Him in baptism, in which you also were raised with Him through faith in the working of God, who raised Him from the dead.
13 And you, being dead in your trespasses and the uncircumcision of your flesh, He has made alive together with Him, having forgiven you all trespasses,
14 having wiped out the handwriting of requirements that was against us, which was contrary to us. And He

has taken it out of the way, having nailed it to the cross.
15 Having disarmed principalities and powers, He made a public spectacle of them, triumphing over them in it. Colossians 2:11-15 NKJV

"Having *nailed it to His Cross"* is a reference to a benevolent practice which originated in the ancient Biblical world. When certain people were burdened down with a debt which could tear up their family, they sought relief from some benevolent individual or individuals in the community. On the gates of the city, one would post their debts hoping for kindness from relatives or strangers. The practice of the Kinsmen Redeemer which was implemented by the Most High God gave the debtors hope that they could be rescued from possibly being thrown into prison by their debtees until the debt was worked off.

The distant relative or close neighbor who decided to pay off the debt would remove the posting from the city gate, put his or her mark on it and then nail it to the debtor's door marked [Paid in Full!] The person paying off the debt could become the replacement debtee or simply pay it off and walk away never to mention it again. Redeemed free of sin?

8 Therefore He says: "When He ascended on high, He

*led captivity captive, And gave gifts to men."
9 (Now this, "He ascended" – what does it mean but
that He also first descended into the lower parts of
the earth?*   Ephesians 4:8-9 NKJV

GLORY! GLORY! GLORY!

Paid in full by Jesus' cross?

GLORY! GLORY! GLORY!

We were in a debtors' prison called the sin nature
with no hope of working off our debt ever. No hope
of sacrificing ourselves enough times on a cross to
payoff that debt existed. The debt had to be paid by
a human with a pure spirit core who also possessed
the nature of divinity.   The power of an endless life.
(Hebrews 7:16)   A spirit core so pure and perfect
that even if this person died under the curse of
hanging on a tree [Deuteronomy 21:23/Galatians
3:13], that spirit core would be so pure, divine, and
full of life that the resurrection of that spirit, soul, and
body would blow the lid off the coffin, the stone off
the sarcophagus, and the boulder off the tomb.

Jesus accomplished His mission in paying for our sin
debt and in the exchange [transaction] permanently
credited our spiritual accounts with His righteousness,

peace, justification, exoneration, sanctification, grace, and redemption. Almighty Most High God implemented that curse just to get His Son into Hell and right in the center of the kingdom of darkness so that He could not only be exonerated Himself as innocent, justified, and righteous but He could rescue those Old Testament souls whose un-exchanged sin nature held them captive in a purgatory type (Psalm 68:18/Ephesians 4:8) waiting area known as Paradise but also referred to as *the great congregation* in some obscure references and portions of scripture which are possibly Messianic predictions.

5 having predestined us to adoption as sons by Jesus Christ to Himself, according to the good pleasure of His will,
6 to the praise of the glory of His grace, by which He made us accepted in the Beloved.
7 In Him we have redemption through His blood, the forgiveness of sins, according to the riches of His grace
8 which He made to abound toward us in all wisdom and prudence,
9 having made known to us the mystery of His will, according to His good pleasure which He purposed in Himself,
10 that in the dispensation of the fullness of the times He might gather together in one all things in

Christ, both which are in heaven and which are on earth – in Him.　　　　　Ephesians 1:5-10 NKJV

Jesus' blood redeemed the past saints, sanctifies the present believers (1st Corinthians 1:30) and converts the future sinners (Hebrews 10:14).　　The past, present, and future sin debt paid in full by the blood of Yeshua Jesus and it was done through WAR.　Jesus defeated the armies of darkness, rescued humanity's souls, and then threw a victory celebration parade.

15 Having disarmed principalities and powers, He made a public spectacle of them, triumphing over them in it.　　　　　Colossians 2:15 NKJV

The public spectacle which is referenced by verse 15 above pertains to the customary trump [abbreviation for "*triumph over*"] processional. Jesus trumped the powers of darkness and Hell on their own turf. The Trump Processional was a celebration in which defeated armies and kings were subjected to humiliation by the victors.　In some cases, the defeated kings were dragged behind a donkey or horse completely naked with his hands bound.　To keep from getting dragged on the ground they had to keep up with the with the animal's pace.　We see an example of a Trump Processional in the tenth chapter of the book of Joshua.　The defeated kings of the

Amorites were executed by Joshua after the armies had been defeated and completely destroyed. Before the kings were executed, Joshua humiliated them by having all of his troop leaders put their feet on the necks of the kings.

22 Then Joshua said, "Open the mouth of the cave, and bring out those five kings to me from the cave."
23 And they did so, and brought out those five kings to him from the cave: the king of Jerusalem, the king of Hebron, the king of Jarmuth, the king of Lachish, and the king of Eglon.
24 So it was, when they brought out those kings to Joshua, that Joshua called for all the men of Israel, and said to the captains of the men of war who went with him, "Come near, put your feet on the necks of these kings." And they drew near and put their feet on their necks.
25 Then Joshua said to them, "Do not be afraid, nor be dismayed; be strong and of good courage, for thus the Lord will do to all your enemies against whom you fight."
26 And afterward Joshua struck them and killed them, and hanged them on five trees; and they were hanging on the trees until evening.
27 So it was at the time of the going down of the sun that Joshua commanded, and they took them down from the trees, cast them into the cave where they had

been hidden, and laid large stones against the cave's mouth, which remain until this very day.

Joshua 10:22-27

In the same way, Jesus Himself paraded the defeated generals of the kingdom of darkness along with their dark lord and stripped them of all their stripes, power, and authority. Jesus' Trump Processional included the complete defeat, humiliation, and degradation of our former captives. He proclaimed it with," ALL POWER is given unto me in Heaven and in earth...." Take a look at the next few scripture references which solidify Yeshua Jesus' victory over the kingdom of darkness. A victory which saved, rescued, redeemed us from the coming judgment of Almighty Most High God on the sin nature.

68 "Praise the Lord, the God of Israel, because he has visited and REDEEMED his people.
69 He has sent us a mighty Savior from the royal line of his servant David,
70 just as he promised through his holy prophets long ago.   Luke 1:68-70 NLT

This annunciation was before Jesus started His ministry of redemption. Jesus wasn't even born yet. This announcement came once Jesus' forerunner – John the Baptiser – was born and named.

13 But Christ has [REDEEMED] us from the curse pronounced by the law. When he was hung on the cross, he took upon himself the curse for our wrongdoing. For it is written in the Scriptures, "Cursed is everyone who is hung on a tree."
14 Through Christ Jesus, God has blessed the Gentiles with the same blessing he promised to Abraham, so that we who are believers might receive the promised Holy Spirit through faith.

Galatians 3:13-14 NLT

Jesus took into His own body, soul, and spirit the iniquity and sin of us all according to Isaiah 53:6. Jesus willingly took the curse and had it punished in Him so that we could be curse-free and never have to be punished for our own sins. No, it is not fair but He put this plan together Himself. The realization of that makes you want to live better, not worse. Too many times I have heard people argue that the teaching of grace leads to people wanting to sin more and get away with it. When you understand that sinning willingly is like whipping, stabbing, and nailing Jesus to a cross again; it doesn't make you want to sin more but sin less. When you realize how much Jesus has done to redeem you, how much Jesus has suffered to redeem you, and that He remains the Lamb of God punished in your place; it changes everything.

21 Through Christ you have come to trust in God. And you have placed your faith and hope in God because he raised Christ from the dead and gave him great glory.

22 You were cleansed from your sins when you obeyed the truth, so now you must show sincere love to each other as brothers and sisters. Love each other deeply with all your heart.

23 For you have been born again, [REDEEMED] but not to a life that will quickly end. Your new life will last forever because it comes from the eternal, living Word of God.   1 Peter 1:21-23 NLT

Jesus' victory in the Redemption War bought us back from everlasting death which the sin nature earned (Romans 6:23) and bestowed the gift of everlasting life upon all who receive the charis [grace-gift] of *The Cross.*

9 And they sang a new song with these words: "You are worthy to take the scroll and break its seals and open it. For you were slaughtered, and your blood has [REDEEMED] people for God from every tribe and language and people and nation.

10 And you have caused them to become a Kingdom of priests for our God. And they will reign on the earth."   Revelation 5:9-10 NLT

Your Enemy The Devil And The Grace Of War

8 Be sober, be [alert]*; because your adversary the devil walks about like a roaring lion, seeking whom he may devour.*
9 Resist him, steadfast in the faith, knowing that the same sufferings are experienced by your brotherhood in the world.   1 Peter 5:8-9

The grace of WAR? In what possible way can WAR be gracious?   In the second and sixth chapter of the Old Testament book of Joshua, we begin learning about a brothel Madam named Rahab whose business was located in the fortified city of Jericho. According to the last chapter of the book of Deuteronomy, the valley of Jericho was adorned with a significant amount of palm trees which were grew date fruit.   Some scholars have dated Jericho's founding back as far as 9000 B.C.   The "oldest profession in the world" located in one of the oldest inhabited cities in history.   Rahab is commonly referred to as a prostitute but not so fast.   Rahab's house was built into the fortress wall of the city. Real estate didn't get much more prime than that. She was much more than a prostitute. Maybe a Madam as previously mentioned and possibly even a coerced sex trade victim. She was under surveillance by the military government for control rather than protection. The King's people knew immediately when the Hebrew spies entered Rahab's house.   She learned how to adapt and make the best of her dire situation. Some twenty or so years ago, I read an archaeological article which cited a study of the fossils from Jericho in which signs of syphilis was found in the animal bones.   IF the men gave syphilis to the animals...is there any wonder why Rahab was so excited to see and help the Hebrew spies?   They were her way out of that hole.

9 "I know perfectly well that your God is going to give my country to you," she told them. "We are all afraid of you; everyone is terrified if the word Israel is even mentioned.
10 For we have heard how the Lord made a path through the Red Sea for you when you left Egypt! And we know what you did to Sihon and Og, the two Amorite kings east of the Jordan, and how you ruined their land and completely destroyed their people.
11 No wonder we are afraid of you! No one has any fight left in him after hearing things like that, for your God is the supreme God of heaven, not just an [IDOL] ordinary god.
12-13 Now I beg for this one thing: Swear to me by

the sacred name of your God that when Jericho is conquered you will let me live, along with my father and mother, my brothers and sisters, and all their families. This is only fair after the way I have helped you." Joshua 2:8-12 TLB

In a culture where some of the worse human depravity was the order of the day, a "prostitute" imagines freedom and finds hope in the stories of the exploits of Almighty Most High God on behalf of the former Egyptian slaves. And she and her family were redeemed from that putrid existence by WAR. Whether you know it or not, you are in a WAR. You may feel stuck in your rut, regret, situation, or hell hole. The good...no great news for you is that Jesus already won the WAR on *The* Cross and in grave for your spirit, soul, and body. It is up to you now. Stop fighting for yourself and accept the victory He has already won for you. Your soul, life, and relationship or potential relationship with Almighty Most High God are in jeopardy of being casualties of the WAR for your soul.

The Final Jihad?

What I am calling the Final Jihad is actually an

onslaught which launched against the chosen people of Almighty Most High GOD in the Garden of Eden. The enemy of human souls was arrogant enough to think that he could leverage the dominion and authority which The LORD bestowed upon the first couple to unseat the King of Creation. The Adversary has injected his arrogance into the human race via the sin nature. The height of humanity's arrogance [proxy demons] will be displayed when the devil possessed leader of the New World Order and his *Disciples Of Darkness* turn their weapons against The Creator when CHRIST returns in HIS splendor to put an end to evil's influence once and for all. Almost.

5 This is the first resurrection. (The rest of the dead did not come back to life until the thousand years had ended.)
6 Blessed and holy are those who share in the first resurrection. For them the second death holds no power, but they will be priests of God and of Christ and will reign with him a thousand years.
7 When the thousand years come to an end, Satan will be let out of his prison.
8 He will go out to deceive the nations...
Revelation 20:5-8a NLT

The scriptures mention a coalition of ten governments leading the vitriol against Israel and anything Jehovah.

These ten governments which would have abrogated their authority to this one world leader will attempt warfare against the Lord Himself according to the seventeenth chapter of the prophetic book of Revelation.

11 *"The scarlet beast that was, but is no longer, is the eighth king. He is like the other seven, and he, too, is headed for destruction.*

12 *The ten horns of the beast are ten kings who have not yet risen to power. They will be appointed to their kingdoms for one brief moment to reign with the beast.*

13 *They will all agree to give him their power and authority.*

14 *Together they will go to war against the Lamb, but the Lamb will defeat them because he is Lord of all lords and King of all kings. And his called and chosen and faithful ones will be with him."*

Revelation 17:11-14

Almighty Most High God will give His Son the green light to unleash the armies of Heaven against the enemies of Israel, the enemies Fof the Word of Almighty Most High God, and against the enemies of righteous freedom. The final jihad will be the last ditch effort to once and for all disprove the everlasting promises made in the Bible towards the Jew and the nation of Israel. Promises made to Abraham, and reiterated to Isaac, remembered by Jacob, and solidified in Yeshua Jesus.

Now faith is the substance of things hoped for, the evidence of things not seen.   Hebrews 11:1 NKJV

The existence of a culture whose language was revived after being dead for over 1,500 years is nothing short of divine intervention. Could the destruction of this tiny nation finally mean that the Bible is a lie? One would believe that only if they have concluded that the existence of Israel and the Jew make the Bible true. That's an interesting subject. What if there is some validity to that theory? What if Israel and the Jew are the *evidence of things not seen?* (Hebrews 11:1) The fact that they have survived threats of destruction since following Abel's murder until now and presumably on until Armageddon is proof positive that Almighty Most High God is who HE says HE is and He is using Israel and the Jew to prove it to the world.

Check out the map on the next page from *iris.org.il* which shows Israel in comparison to the vast Arab and Moslem nations whose total populations outnumber the Jews by at least 70:1. The fact that this tiny nation exists to this day following multiple wars, captivities, and dispersions is an absolute miracle and undeniable evidence that the God of Abraham, the God of Isaac, and the God of Jacob is the One True and Living God.   The dark sliver of a nation under Lebanon on the map is Israel.   Is it possible that the United Nations wants to destroy Israel as a nation to disprove the myriad of promises in the Bible regarding Almighty Most High God's everlasting protection of Israel?

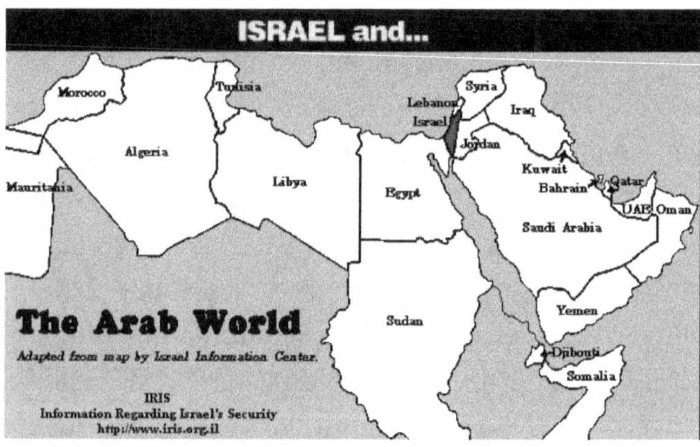

It appears that Israel −"God's Prince"- can easily be pushed into the sea. For the Israeli population to be outnumbered by its hostile neighbors at a 70:1 ratio, been threatened to be wiped off the map, been threatened to be pushed into the sea, and still exist is an absolute miracle.   So many enemies, it seems, should have easily and handily dispatched this sliver of a nation. They were squeezed between an impossible body of water and a hostile military force around 1510 B.C. in the 14th chapter of the book of Exodus. There was no way they could have rescued themselves then and there is no way they can rescue themselves now. The Lord of *The* Rest will do the rescuing while Israel rests, prays, and says, "Blessed is He who comes in the name of The LORD."

The LORD is my strength and song, and he is become my salvation: he is my God, and I will prepare him an habitation; my father's God, and I will exalt him.
The LORD is a man of war: the LORD is his name.

Exodus 15:2-3

Just as Israel has not been able to and cannot rescue itself, none of us can rescue ourselves. We cannot save ourselves. We cannot work enough to earn grace. The debt is way too high. The 18th chapter of Matthew contains Jesus' parable of the Gracious Employer. His servant owed a debt which couldn't be worked off in 100 lifetimes. Repayment was impossible. Hopeless. The servant pleaded with his employer to forgive the debt and the man did. That is the picture of humanity's sin debt to Almighty Most High God. We cannot work enough to satisfy the sin debt. Millions of animals were offered up under the

Levitical sacrificial ceremonial practices.

Still, the book of Hebrews makes it clear that none of those millions of sacrifices put a dent in the sin debt. Even if we attempted to die for our own sins, it would not be enough. We could be crucified on our own crosses one million times and it still would not satisfy the sin debt. Because sin is eternal, the sacrifice had to be eternal. Jesus was the perfect, one, and only sacrifice that could have qualified to satisfy the sin debt forever according to the 10th chapter of Hebrews.

67 Now his father Zacharias was filled with the Holy Spirit, and prophesied, saying:
68 "Blessed is the Lord God of Israel, For He has visited and redeemed His people,
69 And has raised up a horn of salvation for us In the house of His servant David,
70 As He spoke by the mouth of His holy prophets, Who have been since the world began,
71 That we should be saved from our enemies And from the hand of all who hate us,   Luke 1:67-71

Yes, Jesus was sent to redeem His people and He did just that. That is why working for grace is a waste of time and an insult to Jesus' suffering. That is why getting lost in busy religious work for the purpose of finding grace and peace with Almighty Most High God on the basis of our personal contribution is an abomination. The sixth chapter of Hebrews calls the heap of religious busy activity "dead works." Look at Jesus' response to deeply religious people who were asking for something to do so that they can be pleasing to Almighty Most High God.

28 Then they said to Him, "What shall we do, that we may work the works of God?"
29 Jesus answered and said to them, "This is the work of God, that you believe in Him whom He sent."

John 6:28-29 NKJV

"Give us something to do," these religious people said to Yeshua Jesus, "to accomplish the work of God. In response, Jesus told them to simply, "believe the evidence!" The work of God was for Jesus' listeners to believe the evidence of what they already witnessed and heard. Their response to what Jesus said here was to request that he give them a sign to show that He is who they sort of think He is. Why not believe what they already witnessed? Before this discourse, there was the feeding of 5000 men (plus the women and children which accompanied them). Before that was the miracle of the Samaritan village being evangelized by a promiscuous woman who accepted the evidence that Jesus is the Messiah.

Before that was the wedding miracle in which Jesus turned water into wine. With this evidence, the religious people still asked for a sign.

With Israel as the undeniable evidence that the promises in the Word of Almighty Most High God were made by the self same God who keeps Israel in the midst of all her enemies (Psalm 23:5) will not let the apple of HIS eye out of HIS sight.

3 He will not allow your foot to be moved; He who keeps you will not slumber.
4 Behold, He who keeps Israel Shall neither slumber nor sleep.   Psalms 121:3-4 NKJV

The same One who has promised and kept His promises to this tiny nation, has promised guaranteed mercy to those who accept the blood of His Son as payment in full for their sin debt. Because Almighty Most High God always keeps His promises and because Jesus completed His redemption mission perfectly, we are redeemed.

FOREVER!

Chapter Eight

What Is

WAR

Good For?

And I will put [hostility] Between you and the woman, And between your seed and her Seed; He shall bruise your head, And you shall bruise His heel."

Genesis 3:15

What Is WAR Good For?

Africans sold into slavery were redeemed by WAR.

Abyssinia was redeemed from Mussolini by WAR.

Jewish captives of the Nazis were redeemed by WAR.

Potential victims of the Nazis were redeemed by WAR.

Idi Amin's future victims were redeemed by WAR.

Citizens of oppressive regimes are redeemed by WAR.

Victims of human trafficking are redeemed by WAR.

Slaves of the sex industry are redeemed by WAR.

Societal WARS waged on crime redeems the afraid.

Drug trade victims are redeemed by WAR.

Slaves lynched in Alabama for sport could have been redeemed by WAR. Our government wouldn't fight for us.

America's racial terrorism was pushed back by a Civil

Rights WAR of nonviolent protest and legal recourse.

Congregants locked in a works-for-righteousness religion are redeemed by WAR on dead works. (Hebrews 6:1, 9:14)

Spiritually dead human souls have been redeemed by The Redemption WAR. The WAR of *The* Cross.

This list can go on for quite some time. Many wars which we have never heard of have redeemed oppressed and captive victims. Some wars were strategically prevented by a single bullet. What if history's genocidal megalomaniacs were preemptively "retired" before they could unleash their horrors on humanity? President Bill Clinton called the targeted mass murders of Moslems in Bosnia "ethnic cleansing" in press conferences during his reign in office. "Ethnic cleansing" is the progressive's politically correct or sanitized way of saying genocide. How could a civilized person categorize genocide in such a way?

It was reported that there were more than 300,000 victims of Idi Amin's genocidal orders. How many more victims would Uganda have seen if Amin had not been overthrown? How many Abyssinians [present day Ethiopians] would have been lost if

Mussolini had been successful?   How many more Bosnian Moslems would have died under Slobodan Milosevic if the NATO air strikes hadn't put the genocide to an end?   Had any of the victims which were redeemed by a powerful intervening force been asked about it; would they have agreed with Hatcher that WAR is good for absolutely nothing?   If Jesus hadn't gone to war for our souls could we have freed ourselves?

What would have happened to Britain if Winston Churchill had agreed with the majority of his War Cabinet and surrendered to Adolf Hitler? Operation Overlord from American allies helped to stem the tide of Nazi aggression in Europe but the main reason Britain was redeemed from becoming an imperial colony of the Austro-Hungarian Empire was because Britain kept pushing back against the invaders. They fought a WAR unprepared but with unambiguous resolve to "never surrender!" No one was prepared for this WAR. Hitler was amassing his war machine for several years in secret and simply overwhelmed the skies with 4-6 times as many aircraft as any of his intended prey.

If Britain had the weak resolve of the French and allowed the Nazis to bypass them to plunder the rest of Europe; the Nazis would have returned to

Churchill's doorstep again but without the offer for "terms." Hitler would have taken Britain and being emboldened by conquering Europe; he would have visited America's shores and airspace with Mussolini in tow. Nations which fell to Hitler could have been redeemed by a nation or nations stronger than Hitler's Empire. If they had been, do you think they would have agreed with Hatcher that WAR was good for absolutely nothing?   If Hitler had taken over the world as he planned, would Hatcher's song have made it to production?

Why do you think the Brits' non-intervention policy was in place? Do you think they thought that WAR was good for absolutely nothing? Do you think their minds changed when they didn't have a choice? Do you think that they would have regretted sticking to that policy if they had surrendered ("terms") to Hitler's demands being mediated by another monster and made their children slaves of that unholy alliance? As inconvenient and costly as WAR is, you cannot deny that it is good for something. But what if WARS which were not fought should have been? How did the decisions to stay out of those skirmishes change history, bloodlines, and ancestry?

No one came to the aid of the Armenians during the Ottoman Empire's genocide of the Armenian people.

The year before the genocides began, well over two million Armenians lived in the empire but five years after the genocides were said to have ended; there were less than 400,000 Armenians left. Armenians were the first to claim Christianity as their religion a little after 300 B.C. Did that have anything to do with the genocide? They claimed Christ in the midst of a hostile environment. Well over 1.5 million Armenians [Christians and Jews] had been slaughtered by the Ottoman Empire's Young Turks. Would the Armenian population have agreed with Charles Edwin Hatcher that a WAR redeeming them from the genocide was good for absolutely nothing? No redeeming force came to the aid of the Armenian people. A few foreign diplomats and ambassadors attempted to shine lights on the genocide. No one listened or cared it seemed.

No victim of an unprovoked attack or subsequent captivity could honestly say that WAR is good for absolutely nothing. Jesus redeemed the lost captive souls of humanity through WAR and very soon will redeem and rescue Israel with an army the size of which the world has never seen. The earth will finally know everlasting peace following the Lamb of God putting down Israel's enemies and rescuing them through WAR.

34 "O Jerusalem, Jerusalem, you who kill the prophets and stone those sent to you, how often I have longed to gather your children together, as a hen gathers her chicks under her wings, but you were not willing!
35 Look, your house is left to you desolate. I tell you, you will not see me again until you say, 'Blessed is he who comes in the name of the Lord.'"

Luke 13:34-35

Israel which rejected its own Messiah will look at the impossible odds they will be facing. An army of well over two hundred million will be marching in the last days. Maybe some orthodox teacher will remind the nation of Israel of Jesus' proclamation recorded in Matthew 23:37-39 and Luke 13:34-35. Maybe it will take on the form of a national prayer but they will finally pray to Yeshua Ha Messiah, "Blessed is He who comes in the name of THE LORD!"   Jesus will split the sky, unleash the armies of Heaven, and rescue the Most High God's firstborn – Israel and they will finally, as a nation, be redeemed from their enemies.

11 Did God's people stumble and fall beyond recovery? Of course not! They were disobedient, so God made salvation available to the Gentiles. But he wanted his own people to become jealous and claim it for themselves.
12 Now if the Gentiles were enriched because the

people of Israel turned down God's offer of salvation, think how much greater a blessing the world will share when they finally accept it.

13 I am saying all this especially for you Gentiles. God has appointed me as the apostle to the Gentiles. I stress this,

14 for I want somehow to make the people of Israel jealous of what you Gentiles have, so I might save some of them.

15 For since their rejection meant that God offered salvation to the rest of the world, their acceptance will be even more wonderful. It will be life for those who were dead!   Romans 11:11-15 NLT

Israel's rejection of their Messiah resulted in the door opening for the Gentiles to be illuminated by the glorious light of the Most High God's amazing grace. The covenant of grace which was purchased by the Cross and the blood of Yeshua Jesus is the guarantor of God's agape love. God is Love and Love is God according to 1ST John 4:7-8. Imagine the Love which Almighty Most High God is having been contracted or guaranteed to anyone who puts faith in *The* Cross, the blood, and the name of Yeshua Jesus. That means that Jesus' WAR on sin was good for all of us. For anybody who wants to be free.

What do you think WAR is good for?

Who do you think WAR is good for?

Was Jesus' WAR on the sin nature good for anyone? HE understands WAR and, according to Hebrews 4:14-16, HE understands what it is like to be us.

Even you wounded warrior. As horrific and excruciating as Jesus' suffering was depicted in the movie *The Passion of The Christ*, it was much worse. Jesus' wounds were deep, deep, deep. From the outside in [our perspective], HIS sufferings were bodily, mental, soulish, and spiritual. From the perspective of the Word of Almighty Most High God, Jesus' sufferings went in the other direction. They started deep and came to the surface. The greatest human suffering is not superficial is it? Neither was Jesus'.

HIS bodily suffering is apparent and somewhat obvious. You should look for an article where a Medical Examiner (M.E.) explains the affect each trauma had on Jesus' body. It will change your perspective of what real suffering is.

HIS mental anguish of being crucified (slow excruciating execution) naked in the same manner as a criminal who is beyond rehabilitation brought along with it some shame according to Hebrews 12:2 as you would imagine. The original wording of the Biblical manuscript paints the picture of Jesus "despising" [as a righteous Judge] or passing judgment on the shame. But how? He was the one hanging naked on *The* Cross. Yes, but it wasn't HIS cross per se. Therefore it really wasn't HIS shame. HE was hanging in our place on our cross and experiencing our shame. The same shame which unrepentant and wicked Almighty God haters will have on judgment day. The day when they have to drink their own cup of judgment because they rejected Jesus' gesture of drinking it for them in their place. The innocent Lamb of God could pass judgment on shame even while going through what HE was going through.

The **wounds of HIS soul** came from it being offered as a sin offering (Isaiah 53:10) for the salvation of our souls. My soul. Your soul. A glimpse of the sin offering practice of the Old Testament paints a picture of confusion in which comfort and care are interrupted by sharp blade. The lamb being sacrificed had its head caressed as with loving care putting it in a state of ease and comfort JUST BEFORE its throat was slashed and it saw its blood filling a basin which had a hyssop "sponge" in it. The sponge was used to sprinkle and smear the innocent blood of the sacrifice onto the guilty sinners (as well as some temple furniture) for the purpose of covering the sins of the people.

When Jesus' soul sacrifice reached the equivalent point of HIS Father's comforting caress being interrupted by a sharp blade, what did it look like in the unseen realm?   Was it a slash of words or even the quoting of a specific scripture verse such as Messianic Psalm 22:14 where the suffering person says that HE is, "poured out like water," or some other specific quote? When did Jesus' life or life blood start pouring out? Could it have been before the nails and spear? Could it have been before the brutal thrashing by the Roman soldiers?

Jesus was being comforted in the Garden of Gethsemane (grape/olive "crusher") until HIS agonizing prayers resulting in HIM sweating "great drops of blood." I saw this scripture of the blood sweat many times but had no essential grasp of what was being said until I was enjoying an antipasti snack which included maybe eight different types of olives. As I was nearing the end of a small prepackaged container of olives, I noticed red globules floating in the olive oil.   I had never seen this before and checked to see if somehow I pricked myself with the toothpick with which I was spearing the olives. Maybe I bled a bit into the oil. When I realized that it wasn't blood, I looked up the word "Gethsemane" because I had a gut feeling.

Gethsemane means "oil press or crusher" and when Jesus was dealing with the fact of HIS eternal connection with Almighty Most High God being severed or slashed; HE was being crushed under the weight of HIS obedience. The weight of HIS devotion. The weight of HIS commitment to rescue the human race from the most diabolical tyrant, terrorist, and captor of all time.   The Adversary imprisoned humanity in such a prison that it follows them wherever they go. Wherever I go. Wherever you go. This prison is called the sin nature (Romans chapter 6) and it comes with shame, failure, regret, and self destructive behavior to name a few. Jesus' blood was shed multiple times before HE even got to *The* Cross and then it was shed with every wound HE experienced there.   Why was it shed in so many places? Because the introduction of sin into creation makes us hurt and pay in so many ways.

Under the Old Testament ceremonial practices of sin offerings, the blood of the innocent lamb covered the sin of the guilty sinners.

Under the New Testament Cross covenant of grace, the amazing blood of the Lamb of Almighty Most High God doesn't merely cover sin but it washes clean and heals the soul and then the mind of the stain and wounds which sin has inflicted upon them. Aren't you glad that Jesus knew that HIS WAR would be good for something?

Jesus' worst wound of all was the deepest of all. It was inflicted in the deepest recesses of HIS spirit core. Because HE was hanging on a tree, the curse spoken in the 21st chapter of Deuteronomy well over 1400 years before The Cross had to come. "Cursed is everyone who hangs on a tree," was decreed by Almighty Most High God. Why? For your benefit and mine. You'll see.

Proverbs 26:2 says that a curse will not come unless there is a cause. For the Son of God to die for the sins of the world and go to Hell so that we, I, you don't have to; HE had to be cursed. Being cursed would give the Adversary authority over Jesus because a curse from God would be all that is needed to imprison one in Hell. The great problem Jesus had was that HE perfectly kept the Law of Moses and had a perfect construct of mind, soul, and spirit. HE couldn't be cursed based on HIS own deeds, imaginations, and intentions because HE had no sinful bent or sin nature.

BUT if HE could somehow get hung on a tree then

the curse would come, HIS Father –Almighty Most High God- could pour out his cup of judgment and indignation (Revelation 14:10) all on Jesus as punishment for the sins of the entire world (Isaiah 53:6) and all of history. Jesus' crushing experience included being judged for the whole of man's sin past, present, and future according to Hebrews 10:14.

The saddest part of the book of Revelation is understanding the fact that the haters of Almighty Most High God will have to drink their own cup of judgment, wrath, and indignation because they rejected Jesus' rescue from God's judgment.

Can you see why the Gospel of Jesus' Cross will be the basis for judgment day?

The curse of hanging on a tree caused a much deeper wound than the other three because it slashed and severed the eternal connection which Jesus shared with Almighty Most High God (John 1:1-3) since forever.   The point at which that connection was severed may have been marked by Jesus' question from The Cross, "Why my God am I forsaken?"   He referred to Almighty Most High God from the age of 12 when HIS earthly parents lost HIM in the temple to HIS mock trial by the Sanhedrin as HIS Father. For HIM to refer to HIS Father as "God" is quite significant.

Have you ever been abandoned or thought you were? Jesus really knows what it is like to be us. (Hebrews 4)

Jesus experienced it all for you. Even being abandoned by Almighty Most High God so that we don't have to IF-IF-IF we accept the rescue. HE went to the farthest extent to know what it is like to be us. He was eternally connected to HIS Father and spiritually alive. We were already spiritually dead in trespasses and sins [behaviors, deeds, motivations, intents, imaginations, etc.] and HE died spiritually [severed and separated from God] to identify with us and lift us out of spiritual death. Resurrection anyone?

1And you He made alive, who were dead in trespasses and sins,
2 in which you once walked according to the course of this world, according to the prince of the power of the air, the spirit who now works in the sons of disobedience, [children of judgment]
3 among whom also we all once conducted ourselves in the lusts of our flesh, fulfilling the desires of the flesh and of the mind, and were by nature children of wrath, just as the others.
4 But [Almighty Most High] *God, who is rich in mercy,*

because of His great love with which He loved us,

5 even when we were dead in trespasses, made us alive together with Christ (by grace you have been saved),

6 and raised us up together, and made us sit together in the heavenly places in Christ Jesus,

7 that in the ages to come He might show the exceeding riches of His grace in His kindness toward us in Christ Jesus.

8 For by grace you have been saved through faith, and that not of yourselves; it is the GIFT *of God,*

9 not of works, lest anyone should boast.

Ephesians 2:1-9 NKJV

Jesus did all of the heavy lifting from making the declaration of WAR (Luke 4:14-21) the fighting (Colossians 2:15), the abandonment (Matt 27:46), the abduction (Psalm 22:12-13, 16/Acts 2:24), and spiritual death (Isaiah 53:8/Romans 8:29/Colossians 1:18/Hebrews 1:6). HE died spiritually to identify with us on the most extreme level. Why? So that WE could identify with HIM on the most unimaginable level according to Ephesians 2:7 and 2nd Peter 1:2-4.

Jesus went to the farthest extent to identify with us; to know what it is like to be us to give us the opportunity to know what it is like to be HIM.

Completely free.
Completely alive.
Completely whole.
Completely healed.
Completely justified.
Completely righteous.
Completely at peace with your Heavenly Father.
Completely comfortable in the presence of Almighty Most High God.

Just talk to HIM.

Just reach out and take the rescue and healing which HE has already accomplished for you.
Yes Jesus, Yes!

Thank YOU for going through hell and to Hell for me so I don't have to.

Thank YOU for taking my place on my cross.

Thank YOU for taking my punishment for me and for drinking my cup of judgment and indignation.

Thank YOU for forgiving me of my sins and for healing my wounded soul on *The* Cross and for resurrecting my dead human spirit with Your resurrection.

Thank you for healing my mind and body with the wounds your body endured from the beatings and abuse. (1ˢᵗ Peter 2:24)

Thank YOU Jesus and yes, I receive it all in Jesus' name.

Yes Jesus, Yes!

WHAT IS WAR GOOD FOR?

The Roman Road To Salvation

But God showed his great love for us by sending Christ to die for us while we were still sinners. And since by his blood he did all this for us as sinners, how much more will he do for us now that he has declared us not guilty? Now he will save us from all of God's wrath to come. And since, when we were his enemies, we were brought back to God by the death of his Son, what blessings he must have for us now that we are his friends and he is living within us!
Romans 5:8-10 TLB

For salvation that comes from trusting Christ-which is what we preach-is already within easy reach of each of us; in fact, it is as near as our own hearts and mouths. For if you [confess] with your own mouth that Jesus Christ is your Lord and believe in your own heart that God has raised him from the dead, you will be saved. For it is by believing in his heart that a man becomes right with God; and with his mouth he tells others of his faith, confirming his salvation. For the Scriptures tell us that no one who believes in Christ will ever be disappointed. Jew and Gentile are the same in this respect: they all have the same Lord who generously gives his riches to all those who ask him for them. Anyone who calls upon the name of the Lord will be saved.
Romans 10:8-13 TLB

Books By Gerald McCray

God's Gals:
A Woman's Place Is In The Ministry-Case Closed!

Unusual Calling:
The Value of Pain and Suffering

Gerald McCray

House of God or Den of Demons?
Get The "Hell" Out of The Church

Whatever Happened To *The* Cross?

GERALD MCCRAY

The Cross Made *All* The Difference

What Is War Good For?
How To Heal The Warrior's Wounded Soul

From Abel To Armageddon:
Israel And The Jew Make The Bible True

Gerald McCray

ManYouScriptAgape@gmail.com
Gerald_McCray@verizon.net